CW00956881

Dear Catherine
Lots of love
Linda
July 1997.

Tukka

Jean-Paul Bruneteau

Angus&Robertson
An imprint of HarperCollins*Publishers*

To the four women who remain my inspiration
— Aimée, Paulette, Denise and Jennifer

Angus&Robertson
An imprint of HarperCollins*Publishers*, Australia

First published in Australia in 1996
by HarperCollins*Publishers* Pty Limited
ACN 009 913 517
A member of the HarperCollins*Publishers* (Australia) Pty Limited Group

HarperCollins*Publishers*
25 Ryde Road, Pymble, Sydney NSW 2073, Australia
31 View Road, Glenfield, Auckland 10, New Zealand
77–85 Fulham Palace Road, London W6 8JB, United Kingdom
Hazelton Lanes, 55 Avenue Road, Suite 2900, Toronto, Ontario M5R 3L2
and 1995 Markham Road, Scarborough, Ontario M1B 5M8, Canada
10 East 53rd Street, New York NY 10032, USA

National Library of Australia Cataloguing-in-Publication data:

Bruneteau, Jean-Paul, 1956–.
Tukka: real Australian food.

Bibliography.
Includes index.
ISBN 0 207 18966 8.

1. Cookery (Wild foods). 2. Wild foods – Australia.
I. Title.

641.5994

Front cover photograph by Joe Filshie; styling by Georgina Dolling
Flap photograph of author by Nobuhiko Sakai
Page 224 photograph of author by Tim Webster
9 8 7 6 5 4 3 2 1   99 98 97 96

foreword

In 1986, after long sojourns in the beautiful wilderness of Aboriginal Australia, when I was busy writing *Bush Food: Aboriginal Food and Herbal Medicine*, I met Jean-Paul Bruneteau. He served me delicious witjuti grubs with satay peanut sauce and a salad of green leaves from the wild creeks around Sydney. His restaurant clearly served terrific food in keeping with both Australia's history and geography.

Then, as now, Jean-Paul was obsessively and excitedly devoted to finding and *discovering* ways of cooking and treating native fruits and foods to create truly indigenous flavours which would be new to world cuisine.

His great successes are detailed in this book, along with the many errors it took to 'find' the best ways to prepare Australian foods. Many other chefs have followed his lead and a number of Aboriginal communities are now involved with harvesting and producing the foods and plants for the bush-food industry. All should be indebted to Jean-Paul's pioneering work. I am delighted that now we will be able to appreciate his own distinctive contribution and excellent recipes of the outstandingly successful dishes he has developed over the years at his two famous Sydney restaurants, Rowntrees, and now Riberries — the food he calls 'Tukka'.

jennifer isaacs

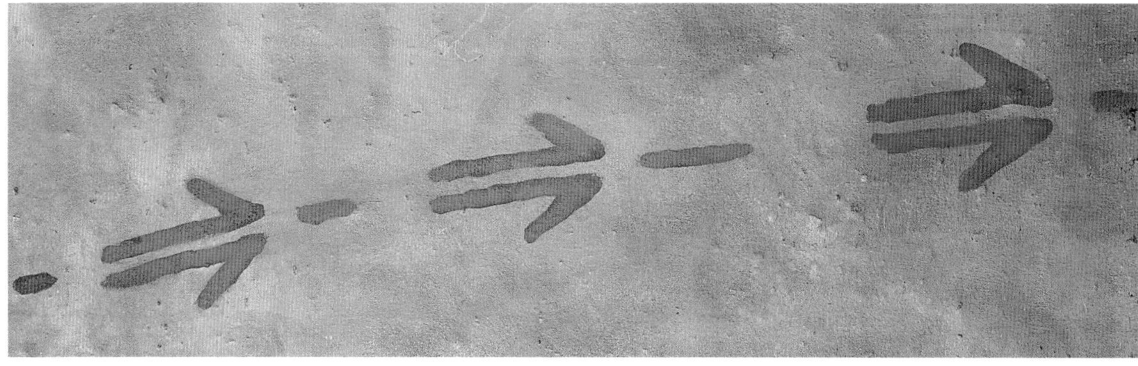

Contents

Chapter photo credits

Page	
15	Illawarra plums. Jean-Paul Bruneteau
25	Section of *X-ray painting of kangaroo*, Geoff Ferguson. Warwick Kent
33	*Tasmannia lanceolata* leaf and loose fruit. Jean-Paul Bruneteau
43	Bunya nut kernels and shells showing colour variation. Warwick Kent
51	Freshly dug-out witjuti grub. Steve Strike, Outback Photographics
59	Freshly-picked quandongs from Mrs Merle Ferguson's tree, cut to reveal the seeds. Jean-Paul Bruneteau
69	Emu, *Dromaius novae-hollandiae*. Steve Strike, Outback Photographics
79	Barramundi, *Lates calcarifer*. Steve Strike, Outback Photographics
89	Cape Barren goose, *Cereopsis novaehollandiae*. Nature Focus Library / Howard Plowman
99	Using a coolamon as a hat. Donald Thomson., courtesy of Mrs Dorita Thomson and Museum of Victoria
107	Gummy shark and ray flaps. Warwick Kent
117	Samphire in foreground, tetragon in background. Jean-Paul Bruneteau
125	Lemon-scented myrtle, *Backhousia citriodora*. Jean-Paul Bruneteau
135	Macadamia in flower. Jean-Paul Bruneteau
145	Native bee honey pots. Tim Low
153	Riberry fruit. Jean-Paul Bruneteau
165	Yabbies, *Cherax destructor*, showing colour variations. Warwick Kent
173	Muttonbird flock. Nature Focus Library / Nigel P. Brothers
183	Periwinkle shell and caps. Warwick Kent
193	Billy-goat plum, sometimes called the kakadu plum. Glenn Wightman, Ethnobiology Project, Parks and Wildlife Commission, Northern Territory
201	*Acacia victoriae*, Central Australia.

Preface

For thousands of years, Aborigines of Australia have maintained their healthy lifestyle by making the best use of a vast range of foods and medicinal plants found on this great continent. As hunters and gatherers, Aboriginal people trapped and hunted game, collected fruit, harvested nuts and berries and fished the bounty of the ocean with great success. Australian ingredients are unique and so are their particular preparation and cooking requirements. Since first settlement, Australian Aborigines have, while walking through this vast paradise, learnt how to recognise and identify these foods and devise methods to process, store and cook them with their own regional diversity. It is illogical to deny the existence of an Australian cuisine. Indeed, this is a discourteous and embarrassing comment for all Australians of past and present generations.

Tukka is, to date, the most accurate guide to the flavours of some of Australia's unique indigenous ingredients. The information compiled in this book is the culmination of many years of experimentation and observation. *Tukka* also chronicles the achievements of a number of little-known pioneers within the bush food industry, whose work must be recognised for the achievement of a sustainable industry from simple beginnings.

Our gastronomy lies in global expectations. With an increasing appreciation and use of indigenous ingredients in our cuisine, the culinary world is finally recognising Australia's valuable contributions. In exploring the traditions and roles of some of these bush foods in the development of Australian cuisine, *Tukka* sets out to expand the frontiers of taste.

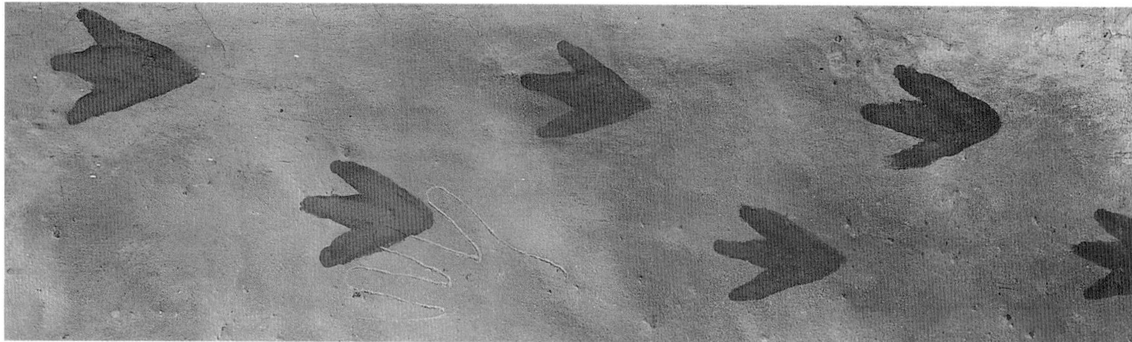

Introduction

My earliest recollection of wild-food gathering goes back to rainy days in France, when my grandfather, Sylvain, and I took great delight in bringing back hundreds of plump *escargots* for Aimée, my grandmother, to cook. The snails were plentiful and very fond of my grandparent's seaside garden. The rain and frequent fogs were perfect climatic conditions for maintaining the land mollusc at plague proportions. It never seemed to be a problem collecting dozens of snails around the lettuces and potato tops. My grandfather always thought of the snails as an added bonus — in his garden they were welcome. Some days later, once the beasts had been purged, Aimée took pleasure cooking them every which way. Pressure cooked with garlic and parsley was one of the most popular, or else they were casseroled, or cooked in grandfather's own red wine. Eating snails at my grandparents' was a full-day affair; nothing else was eaten, and every skerrick of sauce was mopped up with thick slices of bread cut from 'two-pound' loaves.

The wine came from Epernay, Vendée, where Sylvain was born. The family's vineyard produced enough wine for all the relatives, who every year participated in the harvest. None of the wine was ever sold as all of the vintage was shared among the brothers, in-laws and cousins. The tiny one-room cottage standing on the property had been built by Sylvain's parents 100 years before my time. The cellar attached to the cottage used to be the stable. It was dark, and filled with the odour of yearly spills. A deep well provided this modest estate with crystal-clear water, so pure we often bottled it on our visits. Close by, the old apple orchard provided a crop of very sour apples which my mother loved to harvest for her famous apple tarts and compotes.

From the same garden, we picked a type of wild spinach called tetragon, which was much tastier than other types of spinach. It would take me another 23 years to learn that the tetragon I had eaten as a child in France was actually the native spinach of Australia and New Zealand. On a visit to France in 1989, I was jubilant to see it still growing in my uncle's garden. Two hundred and nineteen years earlier, in Australia, the leaves of the wild spinach had been collected by Joseph Banks for the first time. It was cooked and spoken of favourably by the explorers. The esculent vegetable was served as an accompaniment to large freshly-caught stingrays. Banks returned to England with enough seeds to have the Australian spinach propagated in Kew Gardens . Since then, the spinach has found its way into many European countries. Tetragon is a well-established vegetable all over Europe. In Paris, it is sought after by chic restaurants — in Australia, it is only just beginning to enjoy some popularity.

My birth place, Les Sables D'Olonne, in Vendée, is located on the west coast of France, south of Brittany. The beach is famous for its glistening sand, which draws Europeans from all corners for the summer holidays. The 15th century fortified Tower of Arundel overlooks the sea channel there and stands as a reminder of the bloody wars of medieval days. In Les Sables, as a lad, I lived across from the bustling fishing port , where the prime catch was blue sardine and tuna. On most mornings, the rhythmic thudding of wooden crates being unloaded used to wake me. Soon after my mother would be in to open the wooden slat shutters and windows. As sunlight poured in, the fresh smell of the ocean catch came wafting in on the breeze, filling my head with the desire for sea adventures. After my breakfast, a large cup of milky coffee, or sometimes hot chocolate with grilled bread sticks from the day before, I was on my way to school.

Walking along the quays I could greet the fishermen who knew me by name. Their weathered faces read like story books, leaving with me strong impressions. The fishermen were all dressed in blue blouses, with white or patterned handkerchiefs worn as cravates, and they wore wooden clogs which added to the musical sounds of a busy wharf. The majority of the men wore berets which were often flecked with tiny silvery scales from the sardines. Their clothes were impregnated with the odour of fish. Some of the fishermen were the fathers of my school-mates and consequently I was occasionally invited on board their boats to breakfast with them. I relished those invitations. A typical breakfast on board comprised cooked sardine on buttered bread with a large bowl of *café au lait*, much stronger than the one served at home. The men's wives waited patiently on the wharves ready to be given the nets that needed repair. These women, young and old, proudly wore the traditional black pleated garments and tall, white, starched, laced bonnets. Their faces were well tanned and they had spiral locks of hair stuck to their temples with soap. Their earlobes were stretched by large cameo earrings, a legacy from the prolonged stays of Portuguese and Moroccan seafarers hundreds of years ago.

During the summer holidays, at high tide, my favourite pastime was fishing from the big jetty with my grandfather or my uncle. Catching crabs using drop nets was easy and after a day's fishing there were enough crabs to feed the family. My grandmother, equally fond of the crabs, took great pleasure in cooking the sizeable harvests. At low tide, mother's favourite pastime was to scratch cockles and pipis from the wet sand near the fish canneries, where the unmistakable aroma of cooked sardine filled in the air. Aimée worked the production line during the high season and brought home an allowance of rejected cans that did not quite make the check. Sardines, anchovies, mackerel and tuna came back with every shift my grandmother worked. The sardines, cooked with lemon slices in olive oil, were exquisite and still warm from the day's processing.

In the colder months, foraging switched from the coast to inland. Although I detested the long drive to the pine forest, it was not unusual for the family to come back with a basket full of wild raspberries, mulberries and pine seeds.

In winter we travelled further to the oak forest and collected chestnuts from the chestnut stands scattered in the forest. In spring, it was mushroom-picking time in the country. I was not allowed to pick or touch them as only my uncle Pierre, an authority on fungi, knew the good ones from the doubtful. Saltbush shoots were a favourite of my aunt Paulette and were purchased with large bags of freshly-evaporated sea salt from the salt-pan rakers who had stalls on the side of the road. The green Salicornia shoots went well in green salads, and sometimes Paulette pickled them with the gherkins. The young tender shoots were particularly salty and strikingly similar to the type growing in Australia. Paulette, like many of the town's women, spent much of her spare time making preserves, jam and jellies from food gathered wild or bought wholesale from the food market held twice a week in the town square. Most of the people displaying their produce were peasants from out-of-town farms, some of them still travelling by horse and cart.

Up to the age of nine, I lived a life of constant family get-togethers with Sunday lunch being the most 'worked-on' meal of the week. Our house was large and had been in the family for three generations. The ground floor was split up between my father's plumbing workshop and a showroom. The dining room and its alcove could seat over 20 people, among furnishings collected from past generations . Although very young at the time, I still have recollections of the long drawn-out *gueuleton* put on for special occasions such as Christmas, or to mark the numerous religious rites vested upon Roman Catholic children.

My mother, along with Paulette, immersed herself in the preparation of these huge feasts. Lunch on those occasions started around one in the afternoon and went on into the wee hours of the early morning. Paulette, having been born in the house, was usually in charge of the kitchen and delegated the shelling of peas from their pods and the topping-and-tailing of beans to me. Denise, my mother, normally looked after the desserts which were sometimes made from Paulette's preserves. This collection had everything, from white asparagus to quince jelly. On a few occasions, empty jars of strawberry jam and others were found under my bed. The penalty paid for such an act of wickedness was usually a week deprived of dessert.

In 1965 my parents moved from the big house to a new address and Paulette and my uncle Pierre moved across to the other side of the channel to a newly-built home. The sandy block, close to the open sea, fulfilled my uncle's dream of having his own vegetable garden. Out of the sand, which was fertilised only with seaweed, Pierre grew an impressive array of vegetables. Radishes, celeriac, potatoes of all sorts and beans large and small and of different shapes and colour. This delighted Paulette who in turn was kept busy with her delicious preserves. All the haricots and broad beans were graded, dried and stored away for the winter months. In the garden, a plot solely dedicated to the growing of tetragon received the most attention, as it was my uncle's favourite green vegetable.

By the year 1967, completely by surprise and against my mother's wishes, my father decided to uproot his family for a new life in Australia — a place I only knew of as the home of 'Skippy the Bush Kangaroo'. The cruise ship MV *Achille Lauro* landed our family of six in Port Phillip Bay, Victoria. The six weeks spent at sea strengthened further the desire to live my life on the ocean.

Australia certainly was a different place. The food that we were so used to was nowhere to be found. Perrier and Evian water had never been heard of, and the closest thing to a liver paté was meat loaf! The fish looked different and sardines only came out of cans. As 'New Australians' we felt the glares of others when we set out to pick limpets and periwinkles off the rocks on our Sunday picnics at the beach. Foraging by white Europeans was obviously not the done thing and, as an adolescent, being on the beach under the watchful eye of one's parents only created further personal embarrassment. The only way out of this torture was to find a job. I started work at the Liberty milk bar, cooking hamburgers and filling drink fridges every Saturday and Sunday for ten bucks a shift, 'cash in the hand'.

High school was followed by an easy apprenticeship when I was well trained by two very experienced European chefs, Frank Baker of Switzerland and Bert Wendt of Denmark. Finally, I was eligible to apply for a position within the Australian Merchant Navy. Close to six enjoyable years were spent at sea, the last two and a half years as Chief Cook on board the Australian National Line flagship MV *Australian Venture*. The 85 000-ton *Venture* allowed me to fulfill the lifetime ambition of circumnavigating the world several times. Being the youngest Chief Cook ever to have been in charge of galley on an Australian merchant ship was certainly a great thrill and honour — 23 years old and holding the top job!

The extended shore leave accrued on these long voyages frequently permitted me to fly out of Australia as soon as the ship entered Botany Bay. I used most of this precious time to explore India, Sri Lanka, many of the countries of Asia, and also France on one occasion. On what was to become my last shore leave, I trekked through New Zealand, sampling indigenous food with

Maoris whom I had befriended on numerous visits with the *Australian Venture*. These experiences were enlightening and I began to believe that the reason Australian cuisine was nonexistent was entirely because of the lack of indigenous cultural input in Australian schooling and cooking.

As I set out to research indigenous foods, I became aware that the history taught in schools in the 1970s was far from being the wider view. It appeared that the teaching conveniently withheld information about the numerous atrocities commited by Europeans against Aborigines. Australia teemed with all types of edible foods, yet the early settlers imposed their supposedly superior land-management practices on the country. Consequently, the traditional hunter-gatherer existence was degraded, threatened and partially destroyed.

The total disregard of a civilisation's cultural basis was evident from the theft and fencing of land within traditional collection areas. Unless a food could be cultivated, it was considered to have no real value. Land which once easily supported many families over many centuries was locked away for the material gain of a few who saw no obligation to share the resource. The land once respected and cared for was now exploited and rapidly eroded. Incompetent farming practices better suited to other environments irreversibly changed the face of the landscape.These gruesome stories of blatant destruction were perhaps too shameful to include in the poetically written colonial history. I directed my search to the work of early botanists and adventurers who, in most instances, liked and respected the indigenous people. This respect was reciprocated by Aborigines who were prepared to share their culture. This was the history I was hungry for.

I was convinced that, just as history ignored indigenous aspects, the culinary world also failed to avail itself of the wealth of information, flavours and methods that Aboriginal Australia could offer. I was at this stage 26 years old and resigned my position at sea. Within a year, after a short stint on Bennelong Point in the kitchens of the Sydney Opera House, I teamed with restaurateur Jennifer Dowling to open 'Rowntrees, The Australian Restaurant' at Hornsby. In 1984, we were the first Australian restaurant to attain a listing in the cuisine guide section of the Yellow Pages. The listing did not come without first convincing the publisher that an Australian cuisine did or could exist. The subsequent media exposure brought numerous enquiries and potential suppliers to the restaurant. Having secured reliable lines of supply for a variety of bush foods, many culinary experiments were carried out at our Hornsby restaurant. One thing was sure, bush foods were a world away from the more conventional foods that I grew up with, or those available from the supermarket shelf.

In 1988 our cuisine was recognised as legitimate. Eleven countries met at the Second International Cooking Festival held in Tokyo, Japan, where our effort was rewarded with the gold medal for 'The Most Original Cuisine'. In 1989, the French master chef Paul Bocuse on a visit to Australia, paid tribute to our work by stating that our direction was to be encouraged and that with time our contribution would certainly be seen as an integral piece in the developing jigsaw of Australian cuisine.

Since 1991, when we opened our new Sydney restaurant Riberries 'Taste Australia', Jennifer and I have succeeded in further developing concepts by melding indigenous flavours along with an already existing ethnic culinary diversity. Innovative Australian chefs have come a long way and are currently enjoying a popularity previously only reserved for foreign chefs. The imported chefs , once considered essential for the status of an establishment , possibly hindered the development of a better cuisine because of their often rigid European school of culinary thinking. Our approach is boosted by our ability to relax the disciplines and make use of the prime-quality produce that is the envy of many foreign 'culinarians'. The use and understanding of native food is imperative for the continuing development of an Australian cuisine. The native ingredient is the catalyst.

jean-paul bruneteau

acknowledgments

I especially wish to thank Jennifer Dowling, my partner, and Paul James, my associate, for sharing in my dream. A very special thank you goes to my dear friend Janet Bruce. Her guidance, enthusiasm and nimble fingers made this book a joy to research and write — and its completion a reality.The valuable assistance of Jennifer Isaacs, and her foreword, is truly appreciated.

The assistance of Malcolm Bruce in the area of botanical advice was welcomed, and the years of horticultural work of bush-food pioneers Peter Hardwick and John McCarthy contributed greatly.

Gundabluey Bushfoods kindly provided much of the quality bush-food ingredients needed for this book. The dishes were ably styled by the talented Saskia Hay and photographed expertly by Warwick (Wok) Kent. The tableware was kindly lent to me from the collections of Wendy Lungas, Julie Dowling, Harry Lyle Mitchell, Chefs' Warehouse, Sydney and the Unkai Restaurant of ANA Hotel, Sydney.

I thank Fitzroy Boulting, my agent, for his great advice, dedicated effort and direction.

Along the way, invaluable help has been given by Tim Low, Steve Strike, Juleigh Robins, Ian Robins, Bruce Mackney, George and Elizabeth Rakusan, Merle Ferguson, Rene Townsend, Sally Butcher, Annie Reynolds, John Newton, Jean Edgecombe, Mark Peverill, Ian Farquhar, Irynej Skira, John West, Tim Webster, Judy Walker, Chris Rhodes, Denis Archer, Rosemary Cullen-Archer, James Vandepeer, Sharon Glover, Helen Jones, Nick Chlebnikowski, Mike Nash, Brian Woods, Glenn Wightman, Stephen Harris, Chris Harris, Janette Brand-Miller, Mrs Dorita Thomson, Geoff Ferguson, Christine Hiller, Ruth Eeles, Simon Eeles and Margaret Rose.

Additionally, I would like to thank *4 Wheeler Australia* for giving me the opportunity to pen *Potyanambe*, which was the spark of Tukka. Present editor, Ged Bulmer, and the inaugural editor, Ian Glover, have extended their support to the cause.

Finally, I am grateful to the following for assistance and access to materials: the Museum of Victoria for the Donald F. Thomson Collection, Melbourne University Press, the National Library of Australia, the Australian Museum, Nature Focus and the Department of Defence, Scottsdale, Tasmania.

illawarra plum

< podocarpus elatus >

The Illawarra plum is the fruit of the Podocarpus pine, sometimes called brown plum pine or Illawarra plum pine. The botanical name, *Podocarpus elatus*, was given by the botanist Robert Brown. The tree stands as high as 30 metres (98 feet) and has a grey and brown fissured bark. The thick, long and narrow green leaves are waxy in appearance. Australia boasts seven species of *Podocarpus* out of the 14 world-wide and these trees are actually more closely related to yews than to pines.

The coastline south of Botany Bay is a dramatic landscape of steep slopes peppered with beaches of golden sands. From the top of the escarpment, breathtaking views of the South Pacific make this region one of the most scenic in New South Wales. On the coastal plain immediately beneath the escarpment, the city of Wollongong sprawls along the thin strip of coastal dunes. This is the ancestral home of the Thuruwal (or Dharawal) Aborigines. To them it is known as *Eloura*, meaning 'a high place near the sea, a pleasant place'.

Crystal-clear water runs through the area, largely as a result of high rainfall and the sheer height of the escarpment. The rainforest growing on the side of the escarpment benefits greatly from the precipitation, as does the magnificent eucalypt forest further down the rock face.

Many interesting native foods are found in this beautiful environment and

Families

William Clarke, survivor of the wreck of *Sydney Cove*, kept a diary during his party's hazardous journey on foot from eastern Victoria to the south-eastern area of New South Wales in 1797. His account describes the Illawarra Aborigines as being strong, muscular people with long straight hair, flat noses and broad thick lips. The men and women were scantily clad and smeared their hair with shark oil or blubber. The men had beards and wore on their temples ornaments of fish bones or kangaroo teeth embedded in gum and attached to string. A bone or a reed was worn through the pierced septum of the nose. The women wore possum-fur cloaks across their shoulders, useful for keeping the newborn babies warm when carried on the back.

In the Illawarra, many of the families lived in the open, in bark *gunyahs* (or *gunnies*); others laid claim to caves carved out of the sandstone escarpment. Every night the campfire was lit to keep the clan warm and to protect against bad spirits.

The Illawarra people recorded their life and beliefs by drawing and painting on cave walls, using ochres and charcoal. South of the Shoalhaven River, the Wandandian Aborigines drew men, women, sharks and tortoises on rock ledges deep in the red cedar forest.

Courtesy of the Mitchell Library

Australian Aborigines hunting and fishing, Coolgardie, Western Australia, c. 1894.

the Illawarra plum is one of the most unusual. In early autumn, the Podocarpus pine droops from the masses of fruit hanging off its branches. The fruit has two parts: the edible plum (which is the swollen stalk of the female cone) and an inedible seed (which sits externally on the plum's apex). The fruits look like bunches of purple–black grapes grouped along a thick stalk. Both the male and female tree produce fruits (technically, cones), but it is the female that produces the edible plum.

The fruit has all the good nutritional properties associated with wild fruits. The plum's juice content is high, and this juice provides soluble fibre. With an energy value of 728 kilojoules (174 calories) for every 100 grams (3½ ounces) and an ascorbic acid (vitamin C) content of 11 per cent, the plum certainly helped maintain the winter health of the local people. The black and white currawongs are fond of the fruit and would have competed for it with the Aborigines. The children of the white settlers soon discovered this tasty treat of nature and referred to the plums as 'damsons'.

preparation of the illawarra plum

The plum has a resinous centre core, giving it a pleasant pine taste but there is also a hint of Shiraz wine flavour. The texture of the flesh is reminiscent of grapes or rambutan fruit. When the fruit is cut across its girth and each sphere separated carefully, the mucilaginous juice attempts to keep the fruit together. When heat is applied to the plum, an incredible chemical process takes place. Over many years of experimentation with this fruit, I have now worked out the secrets of its cooking.

MAKING JAM

First of all, do not attempt any standard jam recipes with this fruit until you are prepared to 'olive pip' the resinous core traversing the plum. If you fail to follow this simple instruction, the intended jam will turn out a dark, syrupy, sickly brew with hard shrunken plums sitting on the bottom of the copper pan. The failed jam will be astringent and will leave a lingering metallic flavour on the palate.

Weigh the flesh after slicing it away from the resinous vein and measure out an equal weight of sugar. Place the sliced flesh and sugar into a copper pan and place on a slow flame, taking great care to stir every few minutes so the mixture will not burn. Your reward will be Illawarra plum jam, glossy and ink-purple in colour, with a 'wet forest' flavour. Ambrosia, as I affectionately call it, will indeed stir the sensorium.

MAKING SAUCE

A wonderful sauce can be made from the Illawarra plum which does not require 'pipping' the resinous stems. The recipe took three frustrating years to develop.

The most natural thing to do with a quantity of fruits is to cook them. When I first boiled the plums in water and achieved a 'metallic brew', I knew I was on the wrong track. I soon realised that this fruit was like a lot of other native foods — that is, it did not lend itself to usual culinary applications.

The next test was to cook the fruit in stainless steel without boiling it. The result was a little more palatable but not by much. It seemed that the Illawarra plum was only really good for making ink.

When the mixture was placed in the refrigerator overnight (as punishment), the cooling of the podocarpus ink proved to be the solution to the problem of the metallic taste. There was hardly any dryness on the tongue caused by the resin, the brew was purple and it tasted a lot more like the real flavour of the fruit. At this stage, I proceeded to reduce the syrup by half and then cooled it over night; it worked as well. There was no residual taste in the brew. Eureka! I had found my way around this wonderful fruit.

a culinary exchange

In 1798, the English navigator Matthew Flinders was forced to shelter from heavy seas en route to confirm the existence of a southern strait (Bass Strait). He took refuge at Twofold Bay, near Eden, on the far south coast of New South Wales. Once the Norfolk Island-pine sloop was safely anchored, Matthew Flinders and a crewman went ashore. On the beach they were greeted by the screams of three Thawa women who were spooked by the colour of their skin. Having been alerted by the fracas, a middle-aged tribal man appeared out of the bushes. Capable of speaking a few Aboriginal words, Flinders offered a rusk to the Thawa man. The Aborigine reciprocated with an offering of warm whale blubber, once he realised the biscuit was meant to be eaten. The two men did not dare rebuke each other's generosity but found it amusingly agreeable that each other's offering was equally repugnant.

Matthew Flinders was 24 years old and about to circumnavigate Tasmania and the mainland for the first time.

The next stage of the sauce was to make a sweet and sour base using half sugar, half white-wine vinegar and reducing that by half on simmer. Then, freshly minced garlic, ginger and a generous amount of chillies were fried off in a stainless-steel pot with butter. (The reason I used butter was because, when the sauce cooled down, it would be possible to retrieve the solidified fat from the surface.) Then, the Illawarra plum liquor and the sweet and sour base were blended and added to the sweated chilli mixture. The mixture was reduced by half again, but not allowed to boil.

This sauce can be thickened with arrowroot for a clear sauce or with cornflour (cornstarch) for a more opaque look. The finished sauce should be stored overnight in the refrigerator and tasted the following morning. It is absolutely pointless to taste the sauce straight after cooking — the resinous feature comes through far too strongly, making it impossible for the palate to make a proper judgment.

So here we have a sauce that needs to cool right down after every stage. The result is well worth the effort. It can be bottled and stored for later use, and it can be reheated — but must never boil. Podocarpus sauce works extremely well with meat dishes. The flesh strained from the purple liquor makes a good stuffing for lamb and acts as a natural tenderiser.

Another great application of this fruit is with desserts. In a fruit salad, it is quite distinctive as an unusual but pleasant fruit. For extra effect, the plum can be peeled by quickly scalding it in boiling water. Spiking a nutmeal tart with fresh or frozen plums is by far the easiest way, and one of the best ways, to appreciate the flavour of the Illawarra plum.

Courtesy of the Mitchell Library

'Jimmy Bigfoot. Australian native carrying a kangaroo to his camp'.
Gerard Krefft (c. 1857–66)
Watercolour 31.3 x 23.5 cm

<illawarra plum ambrosia>

MAKES 1 KG (2 LB) OF JAM

1 kg (2 lb) seeded Illawarra plums

200 ml (6½ fl oz) dark grape juice

500 g (16 oz) caster sugar (superfine granulated sugar)

3 lemons, juiced and strained

For this jam recipe you will need a heavy, copper-based stainless-steel saucepan or jam pan. Do not use aluminium utensils, as these will react with the fruit and give an unpalatable metallic taste to the jam.

1. Wash the fruit after you have seeded it.
2. Remove the resinous core from each plum. Do this by cutting the sides from the fruit, as if you were cutting the flesh away from a mango seed. Discard the cores.
3. Place all the ingredients into the stainless-steel saucepan or jam pan.
4. Cook over a low heat, stirring regularly. The bubbles at this stage will be numerous and small, slowly rising to the top. (A high heat will make the jam bitter and caramelised.)
5. Continuously skim the sugary froth that forms on top of the jam.
6. Reduce the jam until the bubbles are fewer and larger. This will happen after 90 minutes or so.
7. Test the jam for consistency by pouring a large spoonful onto a cold white plate. Allow to stand for 5 minutes. The jam should be thick. If it is too thin, cook further and re-test.

< illawarra prunes >

MAKES ABOUT 500 G
(1 LB) OF PRUNES

1 kg (2 lb) large, seeded Illawarra plums (see note)

Illawarra plum fruits in autumn, a time of the year when the days are drawing in and the sun's rays are weakening. Sun-drying is not, therefore, always reliable.

1. Wash the plums and dry them with a towel.
2. Place plums in a fruit dehydrator for at least 6 hours, at the lowest setting. Alternatively, place them in a 50°C (120°F) oven with the door ajar.
3. Test the fruit to gauge if enough evaporation has taken place. The fruit, when cut in half, should be sticky without being wet to touch.
4. Store in an air-tight container to extend fruit life.

Note: The sweetest plums are those that have just fallen or are late-season.

< illawarra plum and chilli sauce >

MAKES 800–900 ML
(28–32 FL OZ) OF SAUCE

2 kg (4 lb) seeded Illawarra plums

2½ cups (600 ml / 20 fl oz) water

2 cups (250 g / 8 oz) white sugar

2 cups (500 ml / 16 fl oz) white vinegar

1 teaspoon finely chopped chillies

2 teaspoons freshly minced garlic

2 teaspoons grated ginger

1 tablespoon clarified butter

1½ nips (45 ml / 1½ fl oz) Cointreau or Grand Marnier

3 heaped tablespoons cornflour (cornstarch)

This delicious sauce has three flavours. On the palate sweetness is detected first, then chilli heat and lastly the delicate pine and plum flavour. You will need a stainless-steel pan for this recipe.

1. Place the plums and 2 cups (500 ml / 16 fl oz) of the water into a stainless-steel pot. Simmer (do not boil) for 3 hours. Drain and push through a sieve. Cool and store overnight in the refrigerator. This will become the Illawarra liquor.
2. Make a syrup of sugar and vinegar by bringing to them to the boil and simmering 30 minutes.
3. In a separate, stainless-steel pan, sweat the finely chopped chillies, minced garlic and grated ginger in clarified butter.
4. Add the Illawarra liquor to the sweated chilli mixture, then the vinegar–sugar syrup and the Cointreau or Grand Marnier.
5. Reduce by half.
6. Thicken with cornflour blended with the remaining half a cup (125 ml / 4 fl oz) of water.

<illawarra plum and nutmeal tart>

SERVES 8–10

THE PASTRY

300 g (10 oz) plain flour (all-purpose flour)

150 g (5 oz) caster sugar (superfine granulated sugar)

1 teaspoon baking powder

pinch of salt

150 g (5 oz) very soft butter

2 beaten eggs

THE FILLING

300 g (10 oz) unsalted butter

300 g (10 oz) icing sugar (confectioners' sugar)

5 egg yolks

100 g (3½ oz) hazelnut meal

100 g (3½ oz) walnut meal

100 g (3½ oz) almond meal

50 g (2 oz) cornflour (cornstarch)

35–40 Illawarra plums, seeded, washed and dried

The inspiration for this recipe comes from Juleigh and Ian Robins of Robins Bush Food in Melbourne, Victoria.

THE PASTRY

1. Sieve flour, sugar, baking powder and salt into a mixing bowl.
2. Add the soft butter and mix with a 'K' beater.
3. Add the beaten eggs and mix well.
4. Rest the mixture in the refrigerator for 1 hour.
5. Press into a greased and floured 24 cm (9½ in) fluted flan tin.

THE FILLING

1. Cream butter and icing sugar.
2. Add egg yolks, one at a time, and beat in on a slower speed.
3. Add all the nutmeals and the cornflour.

TO ASSEMBLE

1. Place the filling in the middle of the pastry, in a mound, away from the sides.
2. Half sink the Illawarra plums into the towering filling. Do not spread the mixture out.
3. Make a foil crown to go around the flan tin. This will prevent the filling overflowing while cooking.
4. Bake at 160°C (325°F) for 1 hour. Test for wetness at centre with a skewer; if the mixture sticks to the skewer, cook for further 15 to 20 minutes at 150°C (300°F).

Warwick Kent

Illawarra plum and nutmeal tart.

4 Wheeler/Warwick Kent

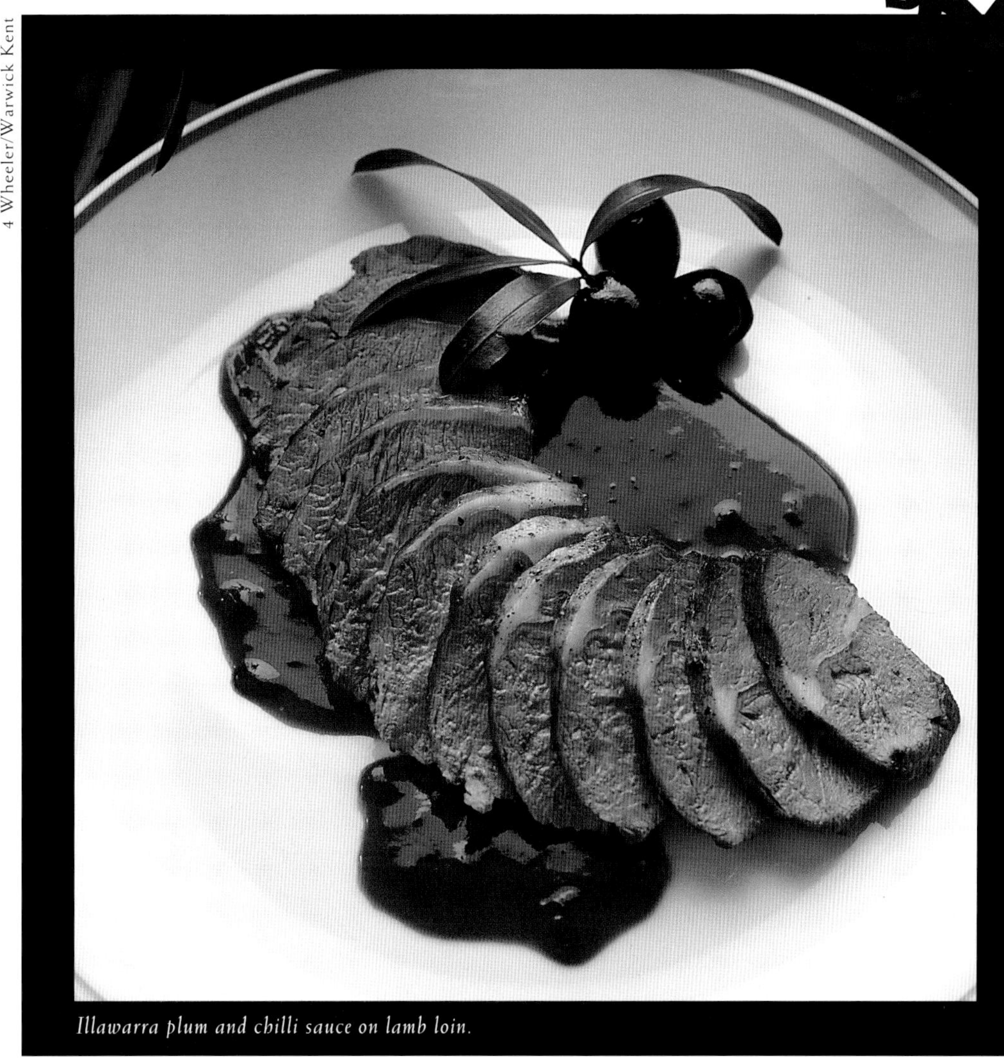

Illawarra plum and chilli sauce on lamb loin.

<illawarra plum and chilli sauce on lamb loin>

SERVES 6

loin of a rack of lamb, trimmed

salt and pepper

oil

Illawarra Plum and Chilli Sauce (recipe, page 21)

1. Season the meat with salt and pepper.
2. Sear in a hot pan with a little oil.
3. Roast for 6 minutes in 200°C (400°F) oven.
4. Rest the meat for 5 minutes before slicing.
5. Serve with Illawarra Plum and Chilli Sauce.

Kangaroo & Wallaby

< macropodidae species >

Along with koalas and emus, the kangaroo is recognised worldwide as one of Australia's icons. Its likeness has been used for trademarks and insignias of many 'typically Australian' products. The kangaroo represents strength and power — qualities reflected in its use as a shield bearer, along with the emu, on the Australian coat-of-arms. Despite the ambassadorial role of its image, the kangaroo itself has been viewed less favourably: from early colonial times, as an object of sport hunted from horseback with greyhounds, to the present day when it has been regarded as being no more than a pest to pastoralists.

Paul James

Bennett's wallaby, Waldheim, Tasmania.

under-valued commodity

The European settlers of this vastly un-European continent undervalued the kangaroo in the wider view of the landscape and the food chain, whereas Aboriginal Australians recognised its value and used it wisely. The recent belated recognition of the good eating quality of kangaroo meat is at last offering the consumer the choice of an alternative red meat that is lean, healthy and highly nutritious.

on foot, armed with a spear

Kangaroos and wallabies are common marsupials with over 50 species in Australia, New Guinea and neighbouring islands. The Aborigines so highly prized the kangaroo for its flesh, bones and skin that they developed unique skills for hunting the animal. Such skills require an agility that has contributed to the physical wellbeing of the people. On foot, armed with a spear, a man can track his prey for several days before even sighting it. Stalking the animal is a highly developed technique. When close to the target, the skilful hunter is able to glide and dart through the scrub until the animal is close enough to be speared accurately. In past times, hunters would burn the scrub with paperbark torches to assist in the capture.

Once the kangaroo has been speared, its entrails are removed through an incision. This ensures that the meat will not spoil on what may be a long journey and helps to lighten the load. The incision is stitched up with a sharpened twig, the legs are tied together with some of the intestines and the animal is taken back to camp.

Success rates when hunting kangaroo or wallaby with spears are low so a kill is highly prized. The considerable effort and skills demonstrated by a young male hunter contribute to his passage into manhood. Once accepted into manhood, the tribal elders pass on to him great knowledge, ancient, sacred stories and rituals.

Donald Thomson. Courtesy of Mrs Dorita Thomson and the Museum of Victoria

Cooking and eating kangaroo meat.

cooking the bounty

A kangaroo is consistently cooked as a whole piece throughout Aboriginal Australia but the preparation method changes from area to area. Some tribes cook the kangaroo completely on top of the fire pit, while others cook it under a heavy mound of hot coals. Some northern tribes use the broken mounds of termite nests, as the burnt mounds retain heat much longer than coals. The common cooking denominator is that the carcass is cooked for very short time. To non-Aboriginal people the very rare meat appears totally unpalatable; to an Australian Aborigine it is ready.

exceptional game

The mainland kangaroo and the Tasmanian wallaby are very lean protein-rich meats, low in cholesterol, high in polyunsaturated fatty acids and iron. Unlike sheep and cattle, the marsupials are not treated with the potent chemicals regarded necessary for the health of introduced grazing stock. The red kangaroo, the eastern grey, the western grey and the Tasmanian red-necked wallaby exist in abundance and are culled for human consumption. This Australian game could wear an 'organically-reared' tag just as comfortably as it wears the red tick of approval from the Australian Heart Foundation.

Like most game meats, kangaroo benefits from ageing. Packaged in vacuum-sealed bags, the export-quality meat improves noticeably in taste and tenderness after 20 days. If a stronger gamey flavour appeals, a further 14 days of storage is recommended. Game meat should not be frozen if practicable. It has a high water content, so the effect is similar to that of freezing and thawing tomatoes — it is just not recommended.

Prior to cooking, the game meat should be steeped in a good-quality oil. This is simple yet essential. Kangaroo meat will not sear well without preconditioning, vital moisture is lost, and greying will certainly occur.

Lenah is an Aboriginal word for the red-necked wallaby or Bennett's wallaby of Tasmania (*Macropus rufogriseus rufogriseus*). Wallaby meat, like yolla (see Chapter 18), is a traditional food cherished by Tasmanians. The meat must be handled as for kangaroo. The red-necked wallaby is not to be confused with young kangaroo which is sometimes referred to on the mainland as wallaby. It is said that wallaby caught in the rough bush is stronger in flavour than animals shot on grazing land. Wallaby meat is a rich burgundy colour, mildly flavoured in comparison to kangaroo and consistently more tender.

CUTS

Kangaroo carcasses are hygienically prepared under the strictest regulations laid down by the authorities. Seventeen different cuts are offered from one animal. In Tasmania the wallaby — being much smaller — is divided into nine pieces.

The legs of both kangaroo and wallaby have the strongest flavour and, because of their sheer size, they are usually roasted. The wallaby tail is very skinny and is only really suitable for the preparation of stock. On the other hand, the kangaroo tail is exceptionally flavoursome — it is excellent in soup with finely-cut vegetables. Frenched racks make great cutlets and are ideal for marinating and perfect for quick barbecues. The kangaroo rump weighs in at 500 grams (16 ounces), is sufficient to serve three people and is best when roasted medium-rare to medium. The prime cut for both kangaroo and wallaby is the striploin. For an optimum result it should be cooked for a short time only in a very hot skillet. This cut is perfect medium rare and sensational rare.

first sight & taste

In 1793 Alejandro Malaspina, the commander of a Spanish expedition, spent a month in Sydney. He recorded that kangaroo meat was 'very good sustenance, inferior to veal, but better than many others'.

It was the Dutch explorer Francisco Pelsaert who, in June 1629, was the first European to sight the Australian marsupial at the Abrolhos Islands off Geraldton, Western Australia. At close inspection Pelsaert wrongly concluded that the young of the animal grew out of a nipple within the pouch. The animal was probably a Tammar wallaby.

<seared fillet of wallaby>

SERVES 4

- 4 wallaby fillets (sometimes known in Tasmania as porterhouse)
- ½ cup (125 ml / 4 fl oz) virgin olive oil
- black pepper

Wallaby is much finer in grain than mainland kangaroo and its flavour is not as aromatic. The texture can be compared to that of veal.

1. Marinate the fillets in oil and black pepper for about 30 minutes.
2. Sear on a very hot plate, 1½ minutes on each side.
3. Let stand for 3 minutes before serving.

<kangaroo carpaccio>

SERVES 4–6

4 striploin fillets of kangaroo (400–500 g / 13–16 oz total)

15 g (½ oz) coarse sea salt

15 g (½ oz) milled Dorrigo pepper

15 g (½ oz) raw sugar

½ cup (125 ml / 4 fl oz) virgin olive oil

Sugar- and salt-cured kangaroo is superior in flavour to beef carpaccio, a raw air-dried meat from Italy.

1. Rub fillets in a mixture of the salt, pepper and sugar.
2. Place fillets on a flat stainless-steel or glass tray. Lay plastic cling-wrap or waxed paper over the kangaroo meat. Place a heavily weighted dish over the meat and refrigerate for at least 36 hours.
3. Pat dry the fillets, leaving most of the pepper in place. Place on a wire rack.
4. Air dry the meat by placing the rack in a meat safe in a cool, dark, draughty location.
5. Dry until a leathery crust has formed. This process may take 4 or 5 days.
6. Store the carpaccio on a rack in a perforated container, or hang the meat in a coolroom or dry cellar.
7. Serve thinly sliced, drizzled in olive oil, with Pickled Billy-goat Plums (recipe, page 198).

Warwick Kent

Kangaroo carpaccio with olive oil and chillies.

< kangaroo tail soup >

SERVES 6–8

- 400 g (13 oz) kangaroo tails
- olive oil
- 1 large carrot
- 2 sticks celery
- 1 large parsnip
- 1 small bulb celeriac
- 100 g (3½ oz) butter
- 1 large brown onion
- 2 bay leaves
- 1 teaspoon finely-ground black pepper
- water
- 1 teaspoon sea salt
- parsley

The smell of cooking tails this way is a little strong, but do not let that put you off this magnificent recipe.

1. Preheat the oven to 200°C (400°F)
2. Run the kangaroo tails through a little olive oil and place them in the oven until the pieces brown all over (approximately 15 to 20 minutes). While the tails are cooking, proceed to step 3.
3. Wash the vegetables, then separately cut each to a very fine dice, 2 mm x 2 mm (1/12 in x 1/12 in). Alternatively, chop each vegetable separately in a food processor (making sure that the vegetables are at least cut to roughly 2 cm (¾ in) cubes before putting them through the processor, to ensure an even dice). Each vegetable is cut separately to avoid permeation with other vegetables, that is, the carrot staining the parsnip, and the onion tainting the celeriac. Keep the chopped-up piles separate.
4. Melt the butter in a pot or cauldron with a solid base, then fry the diced onion. Add all the remaining vegetables, one type at a time, and sweat for 8 to 10 minutes.
5. Place the tails onto the vegetables, add the bay leaves and pepper, and cover with water to at least 10 cm (4 in) above the surface of the tails. If the tails are large, add more water.
6. Bring to the boil, then reduce to a simmer until the meat easily comes off the tails.
7. Season to taste and serve with a generous amount of washed, dried and finely-chopped parsley.

< roast rump of kangaroo >

SERVES 3

- 1 x 400–500 g (13–16 oz) kangaroo rump
- 1 cup (250 ml / 8 fl oz) virgin olive oil
- freshly-ground black pepper (pepper is the best seasoning for kangaroo and wallaby meat)

1. Preset the oven temperature to 225°C (440°F).
2. Marinate the rump of kangaroo in olive oil for one hour or so (overnight is fine — but expect a little of the olive flavour to come through, with a slight discolouration in the meat).
3. Heat up a thick-bottomed skillet on top of the stove — it needs to be *very hot*.
4. Pick the rump out of the oil and place it directly into the very hot skillet.
5. Sprinkle the rump with a generous amount of black pepper and turn to sear all over.
6. Reduce the oven temperature to 200°C (400°F). Cook the whole rump for 8 minutes at this temperature for a medium result; cook for only 4 minutes for a rarer rump.
7. Stand the meat in a warm environment, such as on the oven door (with the oven now turned off), for the same length of time that the meat was cooking.
8. Serve with Pepperberry Sauce (recipe, page 38) and Bunya Nut and Mushroom *Pet-de-nonne* (recipe, page 47).

Warwick Kent

Roast kangaroo rump with pepperberry sauce and pet-de-nonne.

Native pepper

< *tasmannia species* >

Native peppers of Australia are found in mountainous regions, from Cape York in the north to the colder mountain areas of Tasmania. Most interesting of the aromatic peppers is Dorrigo pepper (*Tasmannia stipitata*), which is the once-endangered variety prominent on the north-coast region of New South Wales, and Tasmanian mountain pepper (*Tasmannia lanceolata*), which is found in the high closed forests of the island state, as well as in the Australian Alps region. These are two of about seven species of the genera *Tasmannia* present in Australia, all belonging to the Winteraceae family.

dorrigo pepper

In April 1987, a bundle of leaves along with dark, pea-sized fruits were dried and ground at my former restaurant, Rowntrees. That autumn, *Tasmannia stipitata* made its debut as a rubbed pepper.

Pepperleaf is aromatic and reminiscent of bay leaves (the dried leaves of an evergreen Mediterranean species of laurel tree, *Laurus nobilis*). The heat from pepperleaf is detected slowly, gradually intensifying. The piquant pepper sensation is different from that of other types of chilli-hot plants.

This peculiar native pepper bush grows readily near Ebor in the Dorrigo mountains. Peter Hardwick, an Advisory Officer with the New South Wales Department of Agriculture, harvested the pepper to investigate its culinary possibilities.

Warwick Kent

Dried Tasmannia stipitata.

Warwick Kent

Dried Dorrigo Pepper (Tasmannia stipitata) with handcrafted pepper mill by Ross Pollard, Dorrigo, NSW. The Mill is crafted from a local timber, Leptospermum polygalifolium.

Encouraged by demands for native foods, Hardwick popularised the species giving it the name 'Dorrigo Pepper' which is now the accepted common name in plant nurseries and among 'culinarians'.

Ross Pollard, a resident of the Dorrigo area, is an active member of the newly-formed association for the production of *Tasmannia stipitata*. Pollard hand crafts from local timbers pepper mills designed to accommodate the larger berries of native pepper.

Pepperleaf and berries are collected from private properties, and farmers are now beginning to realise the financial benefits of this native crop that requires no maintenance. The utilisation of *Tasmannia stipitata* ensures its survival and lessens land-clearing practices.

tasmanian mountain pepper

Although the pepper quality of the leaf and berries of *Tasmannia lanceolata* has long been documented, the berries had been largely forgotten over time. The pepper is not known to date to have been of any particular interest to the Tasmanian Aborigines.

The revival in the interest of the pepper bush is largely due to Stephen Harris, Chief Botanist with the Tasmanian Department of Parks, Wildlife and Heritage. In 1990 at the Fifth Symposium of Australian Gastronomy held in Adelaide Harris presented a paper outlining three Tasmanian plants with potential: Tasmanian mountain pepper (*Tasmannia lanceolata*), cider gum (*Eucalyptus gunnii*) and sassafras (*Atherosperma moschatum*). Of Tasmanian mountain pepper, Harris stated 'there is no problem with supply, as native pepper is widespread in western Tasmania'. Subsequently the food media and others published numerous articles on the possibilities of commercialising Tasmania's wild foods.

Diemen Pepper™ is Tasmania's first commercial native pepper enterprise. It is headed by partners Ian Farquhar (an innovative organic farmer) and Chris Read (whose PhD thesis was based on a study of the physiology and chemistry of *Tasmannia lanceolata*). The pair initially harvested leaves and fruit from private properties, abandoned farmland and managed sites leased from the Forestry Commission. In 1995 they had 7000 trees in pilot plantations.

TRIAL, FROZEN ERRORS & HOT PERFECTION

When samples of the Tasmanian mountain pepper's leaves and berries were dispatched to Riberries restaurant in Sydney, several methods of preservation were trialed — inverted hanging of the foliage gives the best drying results. Foliage dried on racks tends to grow fungus while drying the foliage with hot air is too harsh and causes discolouration.

Freezing the berries is not recommended as the fruit suffers greatly upon thawing. The inner flesh severely discolours becoming brown, mushy and malodorous with unacceptable moisture loss. Freezing also diminishes the pepper sensation considerably.

Freeze-drying is an excellent method of preserving both foliage and berries. No discolouration or loss of potency is apparent, however the freeze-dried product unfortunately accepts moisture readily. Until this Tasmanian food spice is commercially propagated and harvested, the cost of this particular preserving method remains unrealistic.

Warwick Kent

Tasmannia lanceolata leaf oil produced by Essential Oils of Tasmania for Diemen Pepper. The green oil stands on a bed of ground pepperleaf.

The optimum method of preserving the berries is refrigeration. Fresh berries must be cool, clean and (most

significant berries

In the autumn of 1993 Paul James, a wild-food purveyor, was inspecting his source of pepperleaf to ensure that his company was not receiving indiscriminately collected plants. He found that the shrubs were plentiful with widespread distribution, and that the leaf's heat quality varied greatly with location. As it was autumn, the shrubs were covered in clusters of black-purple berries. These berries, James was told, were useless to the foliage collectors. He discovered that these very hot pepper-flavoured berries were sensational. The globular fruit split easily to reveal the soft, lilac inner flesh, each half holding a number of tiny shiny black seeds in a central cavity. He was particularly excited by *Tasmannia lanceolata*, knowing that *Tasmannia stipitata* had not long been removed from the rare and endangered list.

importantly) dry for this process. One kilo (two pounds) of fruit stored in a clean, sealable plastic bag and wrapped in several layers of newspaper will preserve beautifully for 12 months at a method is to dry the fruit after soaking it in the brine. Both methods are provided in the recipes for Pepperberries in Brine (page 37) and Sundried Pepper (page 39).

pepper through history

Much of the New World exploration was driven by the quest for pepper and other spices. True pepper, *Piper nigrum*, is a climbing tropical vine that produces densely-packed bunches of berries. However, with exploration, the word 'pepper' was given to any new hot-tasting sensation — pimento, for example (*pimento* being the Spanish word for 'pepper').

European use of genera of the Winteraceae family (to which the *Tasmannia* species belongs) dates from 1597 when the bark of *Drimys winteri* was used to relieve scurvy on board the *Elizabeth*, one of Drake's fleet, under the command of Captain Winter.

Members of the Winteraceae family have long been used medicinally among the indigenous peoples of regions where they occur. The medicinal qualities of the native pepper vine *Piper novae-hollandeae* was certainly known and the leaves were chewed to relieve sore gums and toothache.

constant temperature of 2–3°C (26–37°F). It is essential to maintain this constant temperature to achieve lengthy storage. Berries kept in a refrigerator for 15 months may appear a little dull and slightly shrivelled, but their hot peppery flavour is by no means diminished, nor has the quality of the fruit deteriorated. The pepperberry is a cold-climate species and will easily last the distance.

Preserving the berries for extensive periods of time in a strong solution of salt and water (brine) is a perfect alternative to refrigeration. Another

Warwick Kent

Tasmannia lanceolata berries split open to reveal the fiery-hot seeds.

<pepperberries in brine>

MAKES 8 X 1 LITRE (1 ¾ PINTS) JARS

- 5 kg (11 lb) Tasmanian mountain pepper berries
- 1 kg (2 lb) fine sea salt
- 2½ litres (4 pints / 80 fl oz) water
- 750 ml (26 fl oz) white-wine vinegar

For this recipe you will need a non-corrosive container (stainless steel is ideal). You will also need sterilised jars for bottling the preserve.

1. Wash the berries and dislodge their tiny stalks by running your hands through them. Rinse and drain.
2. Run your hands again through drained berries. The remaining stalks will adhere to your skin.
3. Place the berries in a non-corrosive container and add salt. Mix thoroughly and leave overnight.
4. Drain and wash the berries.
5. Wash and sterilise the jars and bottling equipment.
6. Put the berries into the sterilised jars.
7. Bring the vinegar and water to the boil.
8. Pour the boiling vinegar solution over the berries, then seal the jars.

<pepperberry sauce>

MAKES 800 MLS (26 FL OZ)

VEAL STOCK AND GLAZE

2 kg (4 lbs) veal knuckles

1 onion, quartered

1 carrot, roughly chopped

1 stalk celery

2 bay leaves

5 litres (175 fl oz) water

THE SAUCE

1 teaspoon olive oil

2 tablespoons fresh pepperberries (Mountain pepper, *Tasmannia lanceolata*), or well-rinsed Pepperberries in Brine (recipe, page 37), roughly chopped

500 ml (16 fl oz) cream sherry

1 litre (35 fl oz) veal stock

¾ cup (180 ml / 6 fl oz) veal glaze

To obtain this perfect sauce for kangaroo and wallaby, the veal stock and glaze should be prepared ahead of time. Reducing a skimmed, strained and clarified veal stock over the lowest of heats to a jam consistency is a recommended culinary component of saucemaking, replacing flour or starch thickeners.

VEAL STOCK AND GLAZE

1. Place all the ingredients into a large saucepan and simmer for 2 to 3 hours.
2. Skim. Strain the stock into a bowl. Reserve 1 litre (35 fl oz) of stock and return the remaining 2 litres (70 fl oz) to the saucepan.
3. On the lowest of heats, reduce the stock in the saucepan to 3/4 cup (180 ml / 6 fl oz). This glaze should be of jam consistency.

THE SAUCE

1. Heat a pan with olive oil, add half of the pepperberries and fry a little.
2. Add sherry and flame.
3. Add the stock, then add the glaze.
4. Simmer to a sauce consistency, reducing by at least half.
5. Add the remaining pepperberries. Alternatively, reserve them for serving with the meat.
6. Taste and add salt if required.

<sundried pepper>

These dried pepperberries have a long shelf-life, and can be milled.

FOR TASMANIAN MOUNTAIN PEPPER
(*TASMANNIA LANCEOLATA*)

1. Follow the recipe for Pepperberries in Brine up to and including step 4 of the method (that is, draining and washing the berries).
2. Towel dry the berries, then spread them over a clean cotton cloth that has been placed on layers of newspaper (the newspaper will act as a blotter).
3. Ensure minimal sunlight but a good air flow. The fruit must not be exposed to full sunlight, as it may start fermenting.
4. Test for dryness by rubbing the berries between your fingers. When the berries granulate, after 3 to 4 days, they are ready. Seal in an air-tight container.

FOR DORRIGO PEPPER (*TASMANNIA STIPITATA*)

Simply place the berries on shade cloth, in a warm spot with adequate air flow. This method of drying is particularly suited to Dorrigo pepper. Salt disgorging is not as necessary for this berry, as the fruit is more fibrous than the Tasmanian mountain pepper and does not contain air chambers that impede drying.

Warwick Kent

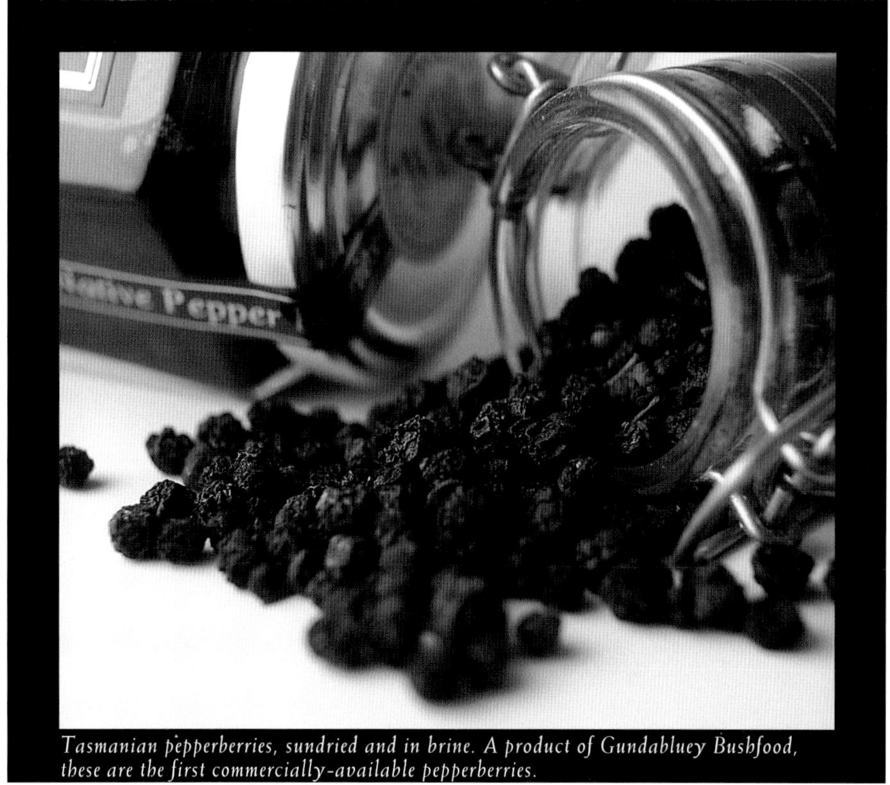

Tasmanian pepperberries, sundried and in brine. A product of Gundabluey Bushfood, these are the first commercially-available pepperberries.

<pepperleaf honey mustard>

250 g (8 oz) white mustard seeds

200 ml (6½ fl oz) cider vinegar

1 tablespoon Tasmanian leatherwood honey

1 tablespoon finely-ground and sieved Tasmanian mountain pepperleaf

1 tablespoon canola oil

1 teaspoon salt

Mustard seeds can be black, brown or white. White mustard is still found growing wild or as a weed in fields of cereal crops in the Mediterranean basin. Although white mustard seeds are less robust than the black seeds, it was the white seeds that were first used as a table condiment. The recipe that follows is inspired by the Mustard with Honey recipe of the Galatian monk, bishop and chronicler Palladius (c. 363 – c. 431).

1. Soak seeds for 24 to 36 hours in vinegar.
2. Crush the mustard seeds and honey to a paste in a mortar and pestle.
3. Fold in the ground pepperleaf.
4. Stir in oil to desired consistency.
5. Salt to taste.

Warwick Kent

Pepperleaf and honey mustard with ground pepperleaf.

bunya bunya

< *araucaria bidwillii* >

But what am I to say about the Bunya Bunya brush? . . .

About the majestic tree whose trunk looks like a pillar supporting the vault of Heaven?

Ludwig Leichhardt

The bunya bunya pine that Leichhardt wrote of so glowingly is a member of the Araucaria family. Within this family there are 18 species, distributed between Australia and its neighbouring islands and South America. The bunya is found mainly in the Bunya Bunya Mountains, a region of south-east Queensland, near Gympie. On the horizon, a bunya bunya pine is easily recognised, growing up to 45 metres (148 feet) and having, when mature, a magnificent inverted parabolic crown that sets it apart from other Araucarias.

triennial food

The leaves of the bunya are spirally arranged, extremely spiky and clustered at the ends of the extended branches. The bark is brown to black, with thin scales giving a pock-marked appearance. The soft wood has an attractive pink tinge. Seed cones are produced each year on most trees, but every three years the bunya produces a bumper crop of several large cones each weighing up to eight kilograms (18 pounds). Each of these large pineapple-shaped cones bears an average of 70 seeds encased individually in a plywood-like shell. The kernel is waxy to touch, cream-white or (very occasionally) corn-yellow in colour and is enveloped in a soft, dark-brown membrane.

Warwick Kent

Bunya bunya nuts in shells.

Bunya bunya pines and their seed cones dictated a way of life for the local Waka Waka and Gubi Gubi people. The trees were called *bon-yi*, the 'i' being sounded as an 'e', and therefore pronounced 'bon-ye'. So important were they to these people that individual tribe members were made responsible for particular trees, and the right to collect the seeds from that tree passed from father to son. The three-year production cycle of the seed cones culminated in a feast that brought together members of many neighbouring tribes. The last of these gatherings was in 1876.

In the writings of Constance Campbell Petrie, she tells of her father Tom Petrie as being the only white man known to be invited to one of these extraordinary gatherings. The 'Bon-yi Bon-yi Feast' was, from his account, a huge picnic where tribal differences were set aside. Tom Petrie was only 14 or 15 years old when he travelled from Brisbane with a mob of about 100 Aboriginal men, women and children. For Tom, the six-day trek from Brisbane City to the Bunya Bunya Mountains must have been the adventure of a lifetime.

Tom and his family had the greatest respect for the indigenous people and in return the Aborigines treated Tom as kin. Constance's grandfather Andrew was the first European to see these majestic trees inland of Noosa Heads in Queensland, in an area the Petrie family pioneered.

Although individual tribe members were responsible for particular trees, the local tribe from the Blackall Ranges happily shared the bounty from these trees. Sharing ensured the inland tribes reciprocal collection rights to coastal foods such as dugongs.

The nuts were eaten raw but roasted nuts were favoured. Nuts which may now be considered past their prime were considered a delicacy, with their sweet 'rummy' flavour and pleasant scent. Often nuts would be stored in tree trunks to attain this mature state.

Dried bunya bunya pine cone (Araucaria bidwillii).

Preparation of the nut

The shell of the bunya nut becomes very brittle when roasted, and because of internal pressure may explode. A roasted nut can be opened by crushing it between two flat stones. The kernel exudes a potato-pine aroma, which complements the delicious taste. If a nut is roasted but not used immediately, it will toughen and become leathery.

When the nut is boiled, however, its culinary application becomes infinitely more versatile. Once the nuts have boiled for about eight minutes, they must be opened while still hot and wet. An Australian Stanley knife is the best tool to tackle this particular task, but the knife must be used with caution.

Fresh bunya nuts can be frozen indefinitely with no apparent loss of moisture. Fresh nuts may be kept refrigerated for nine months with only slight dehydration.

Perfect nutmeal is achieved from boiled nuts by mincing the kernels in a food processor or mincer. The nuts must be left to cool (but not be refrigerated) before mincing. Hot nuts will tend to glug; refrigerated nuts will be tough, resulting in a coarse and uneven meal. Bunya meal stores well in the freezer, retaining its flavour and remaining friable.

Bunya nutmeal is ideal for adding to bread mixtures, flavouring batters and making pastry. Cream is the natural binder, eggs are not necessary, and water does not assist. Creamed bunya nut, using the processed meal, is an alternative to potato and other carbohydrate foods. This same mixture can be pressed into a fluted flan tin as a pastry base for quiches or tortes.

Dark rum provides an excellent medium in which to glacé nuts. The boiled nuts are placed in clean jars and a liquor of very hot rum and raw sugar is poured over. The liquor must be heated slowly up to boiling point, without boiling or flaming. Daily, for 14 days, the liquor is drained from the jar into a saucepan and reheated with a further amount of sugar. It is then poured back over the nuts. The kernels can be stored for up to 36 months in the rum syrup, and are ideal for use in Christmas puddings.

pinus petriana

In her 1904 book *Tom Petrie's Reminiscences of Early Queensland*, Constance Campbell Petrie wrote in detail of her grandfather's finding of the bunya bunya, which became locally known as *Pinus petriana*, her father's acceptance into the local tribe and subsequent invitation to a bunya gathering in about 1846.

Constance believed that *Araucaria bidwilli* was an inappropriate name and in 1906 she vented her rage in letters to the Editor of the *Sydney Morning Herald*. J.H. Maiden, then the Director of the Sydney Botanic Gardens, in a reply to the *Herald* agreed that although Andrew Petrie was the first European to locate a bunya tree, William Hooker of the London's Kew Gardens was justified in naming the tree *Araucaria bidwilli* as an honour to the horticultural botanist John Carne Bidwill.

It appears that Petrie furnished Bidwill with specimens of *Pinus petriana*, and Bidwill — who lacked the necessary reference material to determine an identification — forwarded these to Hooker in London. As there was a similarity between the bunya specimen and a South American *Araucaria*, Hooker required further plant material and Bidwill undertook to collect this and deliver it to England. It was for this dedication that Maiden felt Bidwill deserved recognition.

<bunya nut damper in camp oven>

SERVES 8–10 PORTIONS

- 80 g (2½ oz) butter
- 4 teacups (600 ml / 1 pint) tepid water
- 500 g (16 oz) self-raising flour
- 200 g (6½ oz) finely-minced bunya nutmeal (see note)
- 1 level tablespoon salt
- 1 tablespoon skim-milk powder
- 1 tablespoon sugar

If you can't use hot coals for this recipe, use an oven preheated to 200°C (400°F), reducing to 180°C (350°F).

1. Melt the butter and add it to the tepid water. Set aside.
2. Mix all the dry ingredients together in a bowl.
3. Make a hollow in the flour pile and pour in the butter and water.
4. Cut and fold with a pastry cutter or mix by hand.
5. Warm the camp oven a little and flour the inside surface.
6. Place the dough inside the camp oven and cover with the lid.
7. Bake under hot coals (or in a preheated oven) for one hour. Peep only after about 35 minutes.

Note: The instructions for making bunya nutmeal are in Step 1 of the pastry method for Tetragon and Mushroom Torte in Bunya (recipe, page 48).

< bunya nut and mushroom pet-de-nonne >

MAKES 24–28 DUMPLINGS

1 medium onion, finely chopped

1 medium mushroom, finely chopped

1 tablespoon butter

¼ cup (150 g / 5 oz) bunya nutmeal (see note)

2 tablespoons fresh cream

1 cup (125 g / 4 oz) plain flour (all-purpose flour)

pinch of salt

10 g (⅓ oz) compressed yeast or 1 sachet dry yeast

½ teaspoon sugar

2 cups (500 ml / 16 fl oz) tepid water

peanut oil for deep frying

These dumplings are especially suited for serving with sauced meat dishes.

1. Fry onion and mushroom in butter, add bunya nutmeal, stir and add the cream.
2. Sieve the flour and salt into a bowl. Make a well.
3. Dissolve yeast with sugar in a little of the tepid water. Pour into the well with the remaining water. Add the fried mushroom and bunya nut mixture.
4. Mix thoroughly without over-beating. Cover with plastic wrap and place in a warm area.
5. Allow the mixture to double in size.
6. Using two wet tablespoons, scoop a portion of mixture from the sides of the bowl taking care not to knock the air from the mixture.
7. Spoon each portion into hot oil and cook each side until golden. Remove and drain on absorbent paper. Season with salt.

Note: The instructions for making bunya nutmeal are in Step 1 of the pastry method for Tetragon and Mushroom Torte in Bunya (recipe, page 48).

< bunya nuts in rum >

1.5 kg (3 lb) bunya nuts in shell

250 ml (8 fl oz) dark rum (Frigate or Negrita is good)

250 ml (8 fl oz) dark rum extra

200 ml (6½ fl oz) dark corn syrup

pinch of salt

This recipe should be prepared soon after a harvest of fresh large nuts. It is an ideal way to preserve the nuts for making fruit and nut cakes. The ratio of nuts to rum remains the same no matter the quantity of nuts: 1.5 kg (3 lb) bunya nuts in shell to 250 ml (8 fl oz) of overproof rum.

1. Wash the nuts thoroughly in clean water.
2. Bring the nuts to the boil with enough water to cover, then add rum (as above).
3. Simmer very gently for 1 hour.
4. Let cool overnight in the liquor, out of the fridge.
5. Next day, bring back to the boil and simmer for 8 to 10 minutes.
6. Open the nuts with a Stanley knife while they are still hot and wet.
7. Place the shelled nuts in a sterilised jar.
8. Heat the extra 250 ml (8 fl oz) of dark rum with the corn syrup and salt, add 250 ml (8 fl oz) of water, and pour into the jar.
9. Seal tight.
10. Store for a minimum of 6 months for full flavour.

<tetragon and mushroom torte in bunya>

SERVES UP TO 8 PEOPLE

THE PASTRY

250 g (8 oz) bunya nuts

butter for frying

1 small onion, finely chopped

2 teaspoon finely-chopped rosemary

⅓ cup (80 ml / 2½ fl oz) cream

THE FILLING

1 supermarket carry-bag full of tetragon leaves

275 ml (9 fl oz) fresh cream

2 whole eggs

butter for frying

½ large onion, finely chopped

1 clove garlic, finely chopped

1 teaspoon milled coriander seeds

cracked black pepper

16 medium mushroom caps

salt and white pepper

1 each red and yellow capsicum (bell pepper), baked, skinned and seeded

100 g (3½ oz) matured cheddar cheese, grated

100 g (3½ oz) edam cheese, grated

handful of polenta

½ cup (100g / 3½ oz) grated pumpkin bread

THE PASTRY

1. Boil the bunya nuts for 10 minutes, then open them with a Stanley knife while they are still hot and wet. To make the bunya meal, let the nuts cool and then chop them in a food processor until they are of crumb consistency. Set aside.
2. Fry the onion and rosemary in butter in a large pan without browning.
3. Add the bunya meal to the pan.
4. Add the fresh cream and cook, stirring to prevent the mixture from sticking.
5. Cool for a few minutes and press into a fluted tin.

THE FILLING

1. Preheat the oven to 180°C (350°F).
2. Blanch the tetragon leaves in boiling, unsalted water. Drain and squeeze, chop finely. Set aside.
3. Beat the eggs with 150 ml (5 fl oz) only of the fresh cream. Set aside.
4. Melt some butter in a large heavy frying pan, then fry the onion and garlic with the coriander seeds and black pepper. Add the tetragon, fry a little and add the remaining 125 ml (4 fl oz) of the fresh cream. Cook for a further 3 minutes.
5. Melt some more butter in a large, oven-proof frying pan and place the mushrooms (tops facing down) on medium heat. Season lightly with salt and white pepper. Place the pan in your preheated oven and cook for 8 minutes.
6. Place the tetragon loosely onto the pastry base. Pour half of the egg and cream mixture over the tetragon.
7. Press the cooked mushrooms lightly into the tetragon, face-up and face-down, alternately around the edges of the pastry base. Place the remaining mushrooms in the centre. Pour the remaining egg and cream mixture over the mushrooms.
8. Place the prepared capsicums over the mushrooms.
9. Heap the grated cheeses into the centre. Flatten slightly.
10. Sprinkle generously with polenta, grate breadcrumbs over the polenta and bake at 180°C (350°F) for 40 minutes.
11. Let cool for 15 minutes before attempting to free the torte from the tin.

Warwick Kent

Tetragon and mushroom torte in a bunya nut crust.

Witjuti grub

< xyleutes species >

Insect foods are rich in protein and high in energy with great survival value. This value has long been recognised by the indigenous population and, more recently, the Australian Army. There are several insect larvae known as witjuti (or witchetty) grubs, but the true witjuti grub — the one considered the greatest delicacy — is found in the roots of *Acacia kempeana*, **a wattle known to the central Australian Aborigines as the** *witjuti* **bush, meaning 'the food tree'. This grub is the larva of the** *Xyleutes* **species moth. Although the** *Xyleutes* **species is considered the true witjuti grub, other commonly-eaten grubs are the larvae of the wood-boring longicorn beetle (***Cerambycidae* **species) and the caterpillars of the ghost or swift moth (***Hepialidae* **species).**

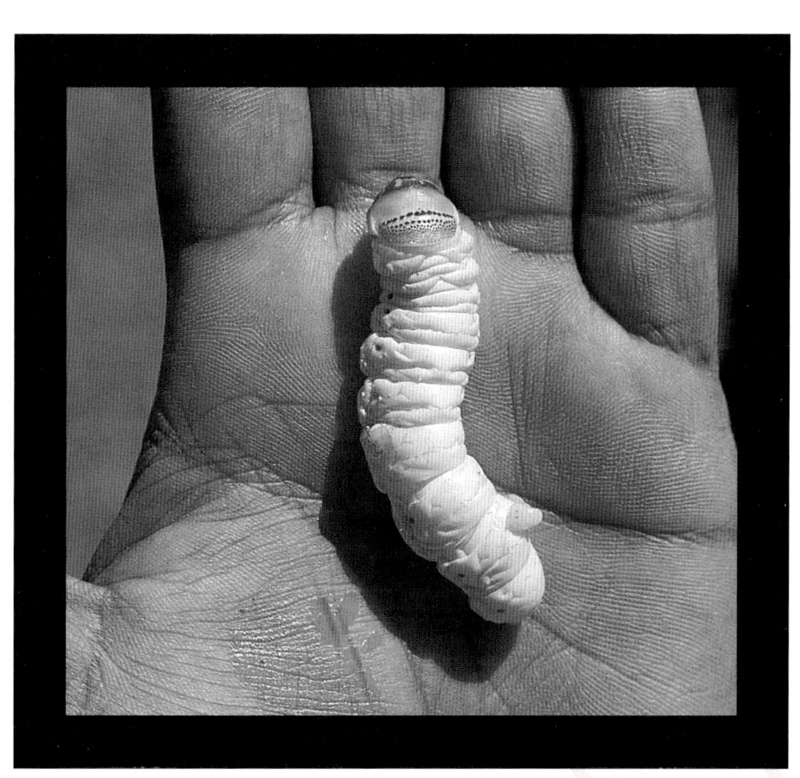

fat grub

The fatty grub is highly nutritious. It is full of protein, provides a good source of calcium and iron and is rich in mono-unsaturated fatty and oelic acids (similar to olive oil). Even after roasting, the grub contains up to 9 per cent protein and 38 per cent fat, with 100 grams (3½ oz) of grubs returning 1760 kilojoules (420 calories). The flavour of the grub will vary according to the host tree. Lightly grilled over dying coals, the lush almond-butter flavour of the witjuti grub is a curiosity and delight.

Witjuti grubs in hollowed branch and on soil.

4 Wheeler/Tim Cole

The presence of grubs in a tree trunk is indicated by sawdust litter beneath the small entry hole. Traditionally the grubs are extracted from the tree trunk using a stalk of the curly windmill grass. The hooked stem is gently inserted into the hole and the grub is effortlessly removed. The flexible grass corkscrews around the accordion-pleated body of the grub and is held firm by the grub's contracting movements, allowing it to be pulled free without damage.

Witjuti grubs are so relished by Aborigines that many are eaten raw during collection. While the women are collecting the grubs they will often give very young children a grub as a pacifier. The grub's leathery hide can be sucked on for comfort while giving the child considerable nourishment. Excess grubs are placed in coolamons and taken back to camp where they are lightly cooked in hot ashes.

the search for the best grub

When 'Rowntrees, The Australian Restaurant' opened its doors in 1983, witjuti grubs were the foundation of its developing bushfood menu. To obtain a supply of these delectable morsels a small advertisement was placed in the rural newspaper *The Land*. The grubs are an Australian curio and this was evident from the attention the advertisement received. Not only were there many offers to supply the grubs, there were also enquiries from a surprised and bewildered media that provided Rowntrees with unexpected publicity for the launch of 'Australian Cuisine'. The best grubs came from the 'place of many brown snakes', Tooraweenah, a small one-time saw-mill town situated near the Warrumbungles in New South Wales. The scattered dead trunks of Tooraweenah's kurrajong trees (*Brachychiton populneus*) are host to large colonies of longicorn larvae. The trees were originally planted to provide cattle fodder and the grubs were largely responsible for the trees' demise.

Unlike true witjuti grubs, which are predominantly sap-feeders, the kurrajong grubs are wood-borers and ingest large amounts of wood fibre. These unusual morsels are as large as your third finger and their body resembles a concertina. The head appears armour-plated, with tiny claws on powerful jaws capable of turning timber into pulp. Tooraweenah grub hunter Bruce Henley reported finding as many as 500 grubs in a single trunk.

grubs on the move

Having located the best supply, the next problem was freighting the grubs by rail. On one epic train journey the creatures managed to tunnel their way through their foam cooler, causing the station's freight handler to remark that in all his years with the railways he had never seen a walking box before. By the time the goods were collected the grubs had broken loose having consumed a box of bush sawdust and demolished the container. A more reliable method of grub transportation was essential.

The solution was to snap-freeze the grubs soon after collection. This method preserves their fleshy and delectable consistency, allows all wood dust to be removed and is considered to be humane. It is far more practical to take the grubs from the freezer, packed in lots of 100, than to chase the little terrors around the kitchen floor!

prize-winning grub

A 'Coolamon Dish of Roasted Witchetty Grubs on Alfalfa Sprouts' won for Rowntrees the Bronze Medal at the International Catering Trade Fair in Sydney, 1985. This was only the first of the grub's prize-winning achievements.

Another Rowntrees' grub innovation was to garlic flavour them by injection. Minced garlic and whipped egg and cream is injected with a large-gauge needle into the already sizzling grub.

In 1988, with the enlisted help of students of Hawkesbury Agricultural College (now part of the campus of the University of Western Sydney), Rowntrees created Australia's first Witjuti Grub and Bunya Nut Soup.

The resulting long-life canned product won for the students the coveted overall Best Food Technology Award for that year. The product was treated cautiously at first, but steadily gained in popularity. One can will make four 'grubuccinos'. Grubuccino is witjuti grub soup served in a demi-tasse, capped with soft whipped cream and sprinkled with roasted ground wattleseed. The flavour is often described as reminiscent of mushroom and hazelnut.

Another prize-winning witjuti grub recipe is a cocktail made with triple sec, crisp oven-dried grubs and a dash of mineral water served on crushed ice in a martini glass. The cocktail tastes surprisingly good, with the hazelnut flavour of the grub coming through.

Witjuti wine with a grub in the bottle made its debut in 1995. Huon Hooke, wine critic of the *Sydney Morning Herald*, described the flavour of the witjuti concoction as 'somewhere between fino and amontillado sherry, and its sweetness level seems almost that of a tawny port'. The wine's nutty flavour is attributed to the grub. The concept belongs to Nick Chlebnikowski, and the wine is produced under the label 'Witjuti, The Original Australian Bush Tucker'.

So impressed was entertainment entrepreneur, Paul Dainty, by this product, that he gave 117 bottles to the rock band the Rolling Stones on their 1995 Australian Tour.

French master chef Paul Bocuse, who visited Australia in 1989, was keen to try witjuti grubs, among other bushfoods. Confronted by the grubs, he hesitated a moment, picked up a morsel, the cameras flashed and, with his dignified demeanour, he proclaimed: *'Vive la cuisine australienne!'*

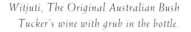

Warwick Kent

Witjuti, The Original Australian Bush Tucker's wine with grub in the bottle.

<witjuti grubs with peanut sauce>

SERVES 12

- 1 onion, finely chopped
- 1 tablespoon minced garlic
- 3 chillies, finely chopped
- peanut oil for frying
- 1 tablespoon curry powder
- 1 cup (250 ml / 8 fl oz) white wine
- 250 g (8 oz) freshly-ground peanut butter
- ½ cup (125 ml / 4 fl oz) warm, boiled water
- salt to season
- 24 witjuti grubs (fresh or frozen)

To roast witjuti grubs the traditional way cook them on the dying coals of the campfire until the grubs are golden. They can also be cooked on the stove top, in which case you'll need a heavy pan.

1. Fry onion, garlic and chillies in a little oil.
2. Add curry powder and stir. At this point the curry will stick a little to the bottom of the pan. Add the white wine.
3. Incorporate the peanut butter and mix thoroughly.
4. Cook until the mixture is hot, stirring constantly.
5. Add warm water to attain a dip consistency.
6. Season the sauce with a little salt if required.
7. Place the witjuti grubs (fresh or frozen) in the hot frying pan with the peanut oil.
8. Using a sharp, pointed knife, prick the grubs just behind the head and at the tail end.
9. Pan fry the grubs on all sides until golden brown, then sprinkle with a little salt.
10. Place the grubs on absorbent paper to drain and cool.
11. Dip the witjuti grub in the peanut sauce, holding it by the head. Tilt your head back and let the whole grub enter your mouth, then bite it leaving the head behind.

< grubuccino >

SERVES 6-8

This witjuti grub soup is served in a demitasse, capped by soft whipped cream and sprinkled with roasted ground wattleseed. The flavour is reminiscent of mushroom and hazelnut.

1. Fry the vegetables in butter.
2. Add whole witjuti grubs and pepper, and cook for 5 minutes.
3. Add chicken stock, and simmer for 45 minutes.
4. Purée soup in blender.
5. Strain through fine mesh.
6. Add salt to taste.
7. Serve in a demitasse, and add a dollop of soft whipped cream and a sprinkle of wattleseed.

1 cup (125 g /4 oz) finely chopped celery

1 cup (125 g /4 oz) finely chopped onion

1 cup (125 g /4 oz) finely sliced leek

2 tablespoons butter

150 g (5 oz) large witjuti grubs (about 12)

black pepper

1 litre (35 fl oz) fresh chicken stock

salt

150 ml (5 fl oz) soft whipped cream

roasted ground wattleseed for sprinkling

Warwick Kent

Grubuccino topped with lightly whipped cream and ground wattle seeds.

<witjuti cocktail>

- cooking oil spray for baking the grubs
- 1 grub for each cocktail
- crushed ice
- Triple Sec
- mineral water
- orange slices for garnish

The grub adds a hazelnut flavour to this cocktail which tastes surprisingly good.

1. Lightly spray the grubs with cooking oil and bake in oven at 150°C (300°F) for approximately 20 minutes or until they are crisp. Cool, then grind to a powder.
2. In a blender place some ice, an amount of powder equivalent to 1 grub, and 60 ml (2 fl oz) Triple Sec. Blend at high speed for 15 seconds.
3. Pour into a martini glass and top with sparkling mineral water.
4. Serve with an orange slice for garnish and a black straw.

<garlic-flavoured grubs>

MAKES 3 SERVES

- 1 clove garlic, minced
- a little salt
- very finely-ground white pepper
- 2 eggs, beaten
- 6 witjuti grubs (2 per serve)
- oil for frying the grubs

If you prefer you could use another seasoning in place of garlic. For this recipe you will need tongs and a syringe (50 ml /2 fl oz) with a needle (18 or 19 gauge).

1. Whip garlic, salt and pepper with eggs. Leave to stand covered in the refrigerator for 3 to 4 hours.
2. Strain the egg mixture twice through a very fine sieve.
3. Load syringe without needle in place, then fix needle.
4. Cook grubs in hot oil on stove top.
5. When the grubs have expanded in the hot oil, remove pan from heat. Using tongs, take hold of one grub at a time, and quickly insert the needle from the rear to the head. Inject while withdrawing the needle. A quick withdrawal is necessary to prevent the egg mixture coagulating in the needle (see note).
6. Cook grub for about 15 seconds turning it at least twice.

Note: It is a good idea to have several needles and syringes on hand in case of blockages. All needles should be replaced in their protective sleeve and disposed of in a responsible manner.

4 Wheeler/Tim Cole

Witjutis in hot skillet.

red quandong

< santalum acuminatum >

From the central west of New South Wales, across to the Great Victoria Desert, four different species of Santalaceae are found. *Santalum* species are commonly known as sandalwoods. A species of *Santalum* not known for its fragrant wood but preferred for its abundant fruit is the red quandong, or desert peach (*Santalum acuminatum*). The red quandong is a small tree with a stout trunk, and grows to a height of around four metres (13 feet). It has a dense crown of pendulous branches covered in matte green, narrow, elongated leaves.

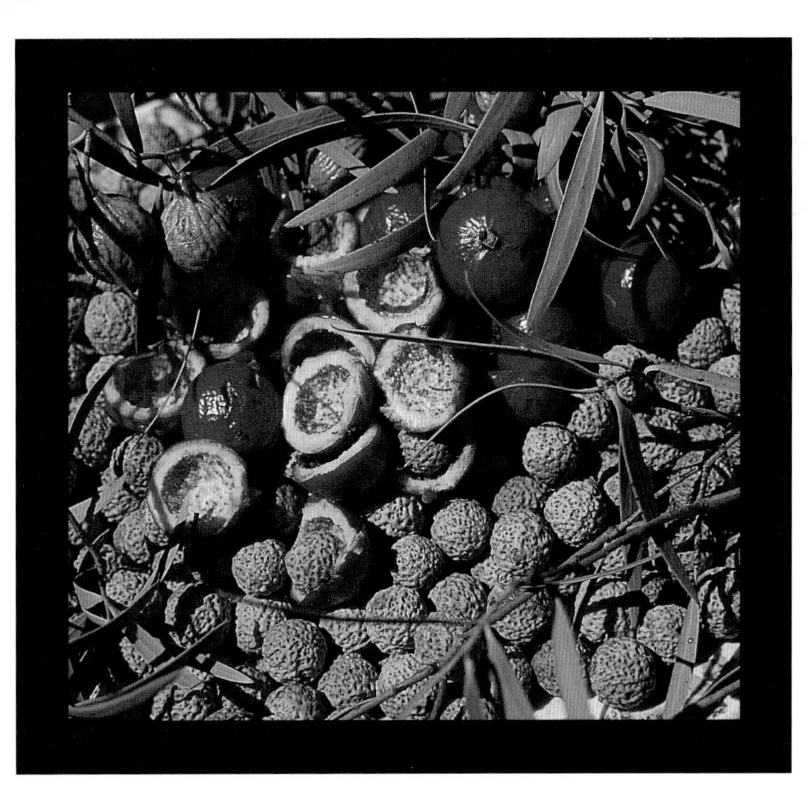

Warwick Kent

Quandong kernels.

The red quandong is semi-parasitic and needs root association with another plant to survive its early years. The host may even be a grass, which is beneficial to the quandong since it does not compete for much moisture. This *Santalum* is resistant to extremes in temperature and will tolerate a poor-quality water supply.

baubles at springtime

The tree is spectacular in spring, when the fruit ripens. From September to October, the ripening fruits range in colour from bright green through to yellow and orange and finally to brilliant scarlet. A tree can hold the full range of colours at one time, giving the appearance of a Christmas tree covered in baubles. While the fruit is ripening the insignificant white flowers for the next crop are already forming. The ripe fruits are 2.5–3 cm (1 to 1 ¼ in) in diameter. They rattle when the tree is shaken and will fall easily from the branch.

Red quandongs have a higher vitamin C content than oranges and can be eaten raw. The flesh has a leathery texture and a tart, yet tangy flavour.

Sun-dried fruit will store for up to 30 years. To dry quandongs, simply cut the flesh around the circumference and then remove the spherical, pitted stone. Place the halved fruit on trays in a warm, dry, sunny area (such as a verandah) for five to seven days. Rain can spoil the ripe fruit, splitting the thin red membrane and rendering it spongy and worthless. The red quandong kernel is 70 per cent oil and can be eaten raw. It is a high source of protein and very palatable when roasted.

guwandhang, gutchu and wajanu

The word 'quandong' is derived from the Wirandhuri word *guwandhang*. The Wirandhuri people of the Lachlan River region in central-western New South Wales used quandong wood to generate fire. A piece of quandong wood shaped like a paper knife is rubbed vigorously across the grooved section of a second piece of wood — the friction is sufficient to ignite a tinder of dry grass or bark fibre.

In the Big Desert of Victoria, near lakes Hindmarsh and Albacutya, the quandong was known as *gutchu*.

The Petermann Range is the ancestral home of the Pitjanjatjara, and here the red and green of the quandongs contrasts with the grey of the acacias.

The Pitjanjatjara people consider themselves descendants of the ancient beings who emerged from the land and wandered over it during the Dreamtime. The harsh climate forced the Pitjanjatjara to adopt a pattern of wide-ranging migration in search of food and water. The quandong is known to these people as *wajanu* and *mangata* and is a significant food source. The fruit belongs to a group of foods called *mai*, meaning 'small food'. The Aborigines dry the fruit in hollow trees so they can carry it with them when food is scarce.

red quandongs

Along Moggiemelon Creek, on a homestead near the Warrumbungle Range in New South Wales, stands a magnificent tree that, depending upon seasonal conditions, produces around 7000 quandongs annually. This tree was grown from a sucker and is the second generation of the homestead's original tree. It has been lovingly tended since 1951 and in 1990 suckered what will be its own replacement. The new tree bore its first crop of 35 quandongs (of the same quality as its parent-tree) in 1995.

These two trees receive great attention and ample water, both of which contribute to the outstanding quality and quantity of their fruit. Property owner Mrs Merle Ferguson tends the trees and records their annual yields.

In the peak season of 1992 Merle recorded collecting 7610 fallen fruit. In a season when rain fell on the fruit, Merle wrote that 'it nearly broke my heart to have to put 3000 in a bag for the tip'.

Merle dries her quandongs on her glassed-in verandah. She notes that it take 8–9 kilos (17 to 20 pounds) of fresh fruit to obtain one kilo (two pounds) of dried shells.

Not all property owners cherish quandong trees as Merle does. In the same season as the rains, she learnt that the previous owner of a nearby property had bulldozed a number of quandong trees when clearing the land. 'Wicked waste,' she said.

quandong enterprises

The semi-arid areas of Australia are ideally suited to the commercial farming of quandongs. The Shoalmarra Outback Australian Fruit Farm run by Ben and Natalie McNamarra is the first commercial quandong enterprise. The 5000-tree plantation is located at Tumby Bay on the Eyre Peninsular, South Australia and produces a fine range of products including dried quandongs, jam, chutney, liquor chocolates and the fruit leather called 'quandong chews'.

In 1988 the potential of this native food was recognised by the Aeroplane

Warwick Kent

Witjuti, The Original Australian Bush Food Chocolates including quandong.

Warwick Kent

Blue quandong (elaeocarpus grandis)

Jelly Company. Rowntrees, The Australian Restaurant, provided the jelly company with quandongs in syrup, along with other native fruits. Unfortunately the jelly's colour was confused with that of the blue quandong (*Elaeocarpus grandis*), a rainforest tree with an attractive blue fruit and fig-like flesh. The stones in both red and blue quandongs are similar, with the blue quandong stone being more pitted and channelled, clinging to a thinner layer of dried flesh.

At present, the quandong is second only to the macadamia nut as Australia's leading commercial native food crop. Although the species' future is assured, the overpricing of the retail stock places them beyond the reach of most.

preparation of the fruit and nut

Quandongs should be re-hydrated in clean cold water for two to three hours. They are best when cooked in the same water, with the juice of oranges and lemons. In September, when the fruit is ripe, blood oranges are available and these enhance the colour of the syrup. Sugar is necessary to sweeten the tart fruit and to thicken the syrup.

Quandongs need minimal cooking over gentle heat. Rapid cooking is not recommended, as the fruit tends to break up and the syrup will cloud. Quandongs are best removed from their liquor soon after boiling point is reached. The syrup is reduced further and poured over the fruit. The cooked fruit will develop their full flavour if left to stand overnight in the refrigerator. This preparation can then easily be bottled for long storage.

The seeds, easily removed by cracking the shell, are best roasted. The aromatic kernel has a pungent flavour, because of the presence of methyl benzoate. As the quandong ripens in spring, the kernel and fruit are timely and tasty additions to the traditional Christmas cake. In ice cream the kernels work better than the fruit as a flavouring.

nature's intentions

Inquisitive emus find the sweet jewels of the red quandong tree irresistible, as nature intended. The emu is the natural propagator of this semi-parasitic species and quandong seeds that are subjected to the gastric juices of the emu stand the greatest chance of germination. The seed is fertilised by the bird's dung and, because emus prefer to shelter under shade trees, the germinating seed will have a host plant. Counteracting the work of the emu are rabbits, cattle and sheep, who find the young shoots of the quandong succulent. This presents the farmer with a potentially devastating problem, for these introduced animals will contribute to the decline of the wild-tree population if left unchecked.

red quandong recipes

<quandong and apple jam>

APPROXIMATELY 1KG (2LBS) OF JAM

500 g (16 oz) Granny Smith apples, peeled and cored (reserve the cores)

500 g (16 oz) fresh quandong halves

1 kg (2 lb) caster sugar (superfine granulated sugar)

4 lemons, juiced and strained

3 oranges, juiced and strained

3 cardamom pods

This recipe is best made from fresh, second-grade quandongs (the fruit that has slight blemishes and is not good enough to dry). You will need a copper jam pan or a wide, stainless-steel saucepan with a copper base and high sides. You will also need sterilised jars and paraffin wax.

1. Place the apples, quandongs, sugar and fruit juice into the jam pan or saucepan.
2. Put the apple cores and cardamom pods into a jelly bag made from muslin cloth and tie it tightly with twine. Tie the twine end of the jelly bag to the side of the jam pan.
3. Bring the contents of the pan to a gentle boil and cook for 30 minutes to evaporate some of the water content, skimming all the time.
4. Bring down to a simmer, skimming surface continually and stirring occasionally. Cook for 1½ to 2 hours until the jam coats the back of a wooden spoon (see notes).
5. Squeeze the contents of the jelly bag into the pan.
6. Bottle the jam in sterilised jars. Cool for 30 minutes so that a slight skin forms over the top.
7. Pour hot paraffin wax over the jam to seal.

Notes: (a) If jam fails to set, reheat gently and add agar to manufacturer's specification.
(b) If the jam crystallises, reheat and add lemon juice.
(c) Jam will ferment if it is cooked insufficiently or if not enough sugar is used. Poor-quality fruit may also cause fermentation.

< wajanu icecream >

SERVES 6 – 8

500 ml (16 fl oz) milk
200 ml (6½ fl oz) cream
pinch of salt
8 egg yolks
250 g (8 oz) caster sugar (superfine granulated sugar)
10 g (⅓ oz) gelatine, dissolved in 3 tablespoons of boiling water (see notes)
80 g (3 oz) wajanu kernels

Wajanu is one of the names given by the Pitjanjatjara people to the red desert quandong. Wajanu ice cream is made from the roasted kernel of this fruit. The kernel is easily obtained by cracking open the fruit's stone with a macadamia nut, or with a conventional nut cracker, but care must be taken to remove the kernel whole. For this recipe, you will need a sugar thermometer and an ice-cream churner.

1. Bring milk to the boil, add cream, add salt, then bring back to the boil.
2. Beat egg yolks and sugar until they are creamy white.
3. Add the dissolved gelatine to the milk and cream.
4. Take the milk mixture off the heat, add yolk mixture and whisk through.
5. Place the mixture back on low to medium heat (or use a double boiler) and stir continually with a wooden spoon.
6. Bring the mixture up to 85°C (185°F) using a thermometer to measure the temperature.
7. Remove immediately from the heat and pour into a clean bowl. Cool the mixture right down before placing the bowl in the refrigerator overnight.
8. Roast the wajanu kernels in the oven at 180°C (350°F) for 6 to 7 minutes, or until golden brown.
9. Cool the kernels and chop roughly.
10. Put the chopped kernels and the refrigerated mixture into an ice-cream churner, and churn until firm.
11. Place the churned ice cream into a sealable container and freeze.

Notes: *(a) The gelatine is optional, but it helps the ice-cream to stabilise its composition in warm environments.*
(b) Ice cream can be made without an ice-cream churner by freezing the mixture into a tray, however the result will be icy and the chopped kernels will all drop to the bottom.

<quince and quandong gutchu>

MAKES 16 – 24 'SQUARES' OR PORTIONS

In the area known as the Big Desert of Victoria near Lakes Hindmarsh and Albacutya, the quandong was known locally as *gutchu*. This recipe is ideal as a sweet after-dinner treat.

- 3 quinces, peeled and cored (reserve the seeds)
- 3 lemons, juiced and strained
- 250 g (8 oz) fresh or hydrated red quandong flesh (see note)
- 3 oranges, juiced and strained
- 500 g (16 oz) caster sugar (superfine granulated sugar)
- oil for coating baking tins
- white sugar (granulated sugar) for coating baking tins
- icing sugar (confectioners' sugar) for dusting the gutchu

1. Put the reserved quince seeds into a jelly bag made from muslin cloth and tie it tightly with twine.
2. Cover the quinces with water, add the lemon juice and jelly bag and cook.
2. Purée the cooked quinces to give 250 g (8 oz) of fruit.
3. Cook the quandongs with the orange juice for 20 minutes, then purée.
4. Pass each of the purées separately through a fine sieve.
5. Weigh each amount of purée and measure out their combined weight in sugar.
6. Place both purées and the sugar in a heavy-based saucepan and cook on low heat, stirring constantly. Eventually the purées will start to dry and come away from the sides and bottom of the saucepan. Take from the heat.
7. Prepare sponge-cake tins by lightly oiling the inside surfaces and coating with granulated sugar.
8. Spread the fruit paste into the tins to a thickness of 1½cm (⅗ in).
9. Put the tins in a cool well-ventilated area for up to 6 or 7 days, until the fruit paste is dry.
10. Turn out the gutchu and cut into desired shapes. Sprinkle with icing sugar.
11. Store in an air-tight container for extended shelf-life.

Note: To rehydrate dried quandongs, soak them in cold water at the ratio of one part quandongs to two parts water.

Warwick Kent

Quince and quandong gutchu.

<quandongs in syrup with sugarbark>

MAKES ABOUT 250G (8OZ) OF FRUIT GARNISH OR 1 LITRE (1¾ FL OZ) OF SAUCE

- 100 g (3½ oz) sundried red quandongs
- 1 litre (35 fl oz) water, for soaking and cooking
- 8 oranges, juiced and strained
- 4 lemons, juiced and strained
- 300 g (10 oz) caster sugar (superfine granulated sugar)

This is an ideal fruit garnish for pies or flans and an excellent sweet sauce for game or fowl. A touch of brandy will sharpen the sauce.

1. Soak the quandongs in water for 2 hours.
2. Put the soaking quandongs in a wide, open pan. Add the fruit juices and the sugar.
3. Bring gently to the boil and simmer for 8 minutes.
4. Remove the quandongs (reserve the syrup) and refrigerate.
5. Reduce the syrup by half on simmer.
6. Pour the syrup back over the quandongs.
7. Let the quandongs stand overnight in the syrup before using.

Variation: To conserve the quandongs, put them in sterilised jars, pour the hot syrup over them and seal.

<sugarbark>

- oil
- caster sugar (superfine granulated sugar)
- raw sugar
- coffee crystals

Sugarbark is a thin sheet of toffee made from sprinkled sugars baked at a high temperature. The raw sugar adds colour and the coffee crystals give the toffee a pebbled texture. You will need a heavy-gauge oven tray for this recipe.

1. Cover the inside of the tray with aluminium foil then use absorbent paper to lightly oil the foil.
2. Measure the sugar in the following proportions: 80% caster sugar, 15% raw sugar and 5% coffee crystals. Keep the sugars separate.
3. Sprinkle the caster sugar to cover the oiled surface of the tray. Discard any excess sugar.
4. Flow the raw sugar in a ribbon pattern over the caster sugar.
5. Make a similar pattern with the coffee crystals.
6. Bake in a preheated oven at 200°C for 4 minutes.
7. Allow the sugarbark to cool.
8. Peel the foil away while carefully lifting the sugarbark.
9. Store in an airtight container.

4 Wheeler/Warwick Kent

Quandongs in syrup with sugarbark.

emu

< dromaius novaehollandiae >

The emu and the kangaroo are honoured as co-supporters of the shield in the coat of arms of the Commonwealth of Australia. Their selection in 1908 was particularly appropriate as both animals have great trouble in travelling backwards — a wonderful symbol for the direction of any nation. It is ironic then that the emu and the kangaroo have long been regarded as menacing pests — a feeling that culminated in 1932 in the Emu War.

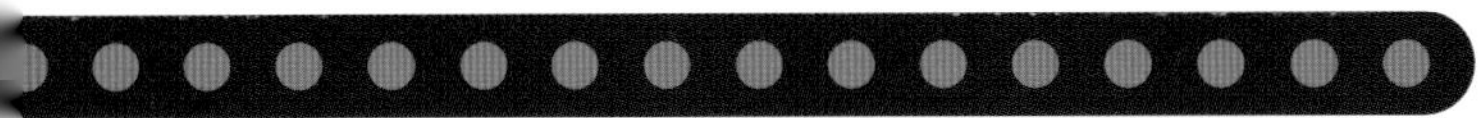

This was a calculated, cold-blooded battle waged against the emus by farmers with government permission. The justifications for the slaughter ranged from the threat of emus spreading prickly pear to the competition they posed to introduced animals. In one district of Western Australia 57 034 emus were killed. The war quickly spread to the east where as many as 121 768 emus died in a two-year battle in Queensland.

In Bass Strait a dwarf black emu once existed on King and Flinders islands (*Dromaius ater*). On Kangaroo Island off the coast of South Australia another dwarf black emu (*Dromaius baudinianus*) was found. Exploration, settlement and the use of fire by the new settlers in these regions managed to wipe out the entire band of these defenceless birds.

oorooba

The emu is found across the continent and is associated with many myths and superstitions. To most Aboriginal tribes, the animal is an important Dreaming creation ancestor. The many Aboriginal names for the emu throughout Australia imitate the guttural drumming sound of the bird: *oorooba*, *koondooloo* and *guraan*. The importance of the emu is well represented throughout Aboriginal life. Emu dances were common in the corroborees, with the men adorning their helmet-like headdresses with emu feathers, or wearing them like tail feathers. Some used foliage to resemble the emu's shaggy plumage. The sound of the didgeridoo evokes the adult bird's call, and images of the emu appear repeatedly in paintings and

Steve Strike, Outback Photographics

Emus in the wild.

Warwick Kent

Pair of emu eggs, one traditionally decorated by Maryjane Mumbulla.

carvings, reflecting its spiritual significance.

The sheer size, numbers and earthbound existence of the birds made them an easy target for Aboriginal spears and waddies. Hunters took advantage of their natural curiosity using shiny objects, waving a cloth or making imitative sounds to lure them into capture.

Water holes also provided an excellent opportunity for capturing emus. Explorer Ludwig Leichhardt noted in his journals that hedges of dry sticks with an opening were used to trap emus. Stupefying the bird by adding the pounded leaves of the narcotic *pitjuri* plant to the water was also common.

Once the emu was killed, the feathers were removed and the whole bird was cooked on top of a fire or in a pit filled with heated stones. The pit method was preferred by the lower Murray River tribe. The bird was buried with its head protruding from the ground and, when steam came from its beak, it was considered to be cooked.

The leg bones were later removed from the carcass and sharpened into knives, while other bones were used to make spear tips. Leg sinews provided strong lashings. Fat from the bird's back was rubbed into boomerangs and other wooden implements as a conditioner and was also relished as a food. Emu eggs were stored in the shade for a period of up to nine months.

emu-farming ventures

The emu is farmed under commercial licence for its meat, its leather and its oil (which is touted as a rheumatic remedy). Farmed-emu products are readily available from game-meat suppliers throughout Australia.

Initial interest in farming emus came from the Swiss partners Kadei and Wuthrich who focused on producing emu leather. Kadei and Wuthrich had studied ostrich farming in South Africa prior to setting up their farm at Kalannie, Western Australia. Unfortunately this pioneering venture closed in 1973 due to low stock numbers and low profitability.

It was not until 1986, when the Ngangganawili Aboriginal Community at Wiluna successfully reared 600 chicks, that emu farming was considered a viable industry in Western Australia. Five hundred of these chicks were approved by the Western Australian Department of Agriculture for sale to stock the new community emu-farming venture.

Emu farming also takes place at Cherbourg in Queensland. This

Aboriginal community enterprise began in December 1988 and ran 2300 birds in 1995.

red meat

Emu meat is dark red and, despite resembling beef, is classified as poultry. The classification quirk is to Australia's advantage because although many countries regulate against the acceptance of game meat they will readily take poultry.

A flightless bird, the emu has no breast to speak of — the leg is the prime cut. The bulk of the meat is found in the legs and the tail and is known as the hindquarter. From the hindquarter the thigh is separated from the drum which in turn is divided into six pieces: the drum strap (which is the smallest muscle), the inside drum, the inner outside drum, the inner mid drum, the mid drum, and the outside drum (the larger pieces).

Eight separate muscles are currently marketed from the thigh, sometimes called the rump: the inside fillet (the inside surface of the pelvis), the fan fillet (which is a sought-after cut, being less sinewy and more tender than the other muscles), the oyster fillet, the flat fillet, the outside fillet, the round, the full rump, and the flat rump.

From the forequarter, which is really just the ribcage minus the neck and head, comes the striploin (a small piece of meat running the length of the forequarter).

The fancy meats from an emu are its heart, gizzard and its healthy-looking liver which is extremely good eating. The neck makes a reasonable stew, although the intricate neck vertebrae makes it difficult to cut.

Emu meat has all the health and nutritional qualities of other Australian game meat. The meat is very low in fat — its total content varies between 1.7 and 4.5 per cent. In a typical nutritional analysis, emu rates better than venison. The tenderness and texture of the meat makes it suitable for a variety of cooking styles ranging from stir-fries to roasting. The meat should not be frozen as it is very low in fat, and great care must be taken not to overcook it.

Warwick Kent

The emu eggs collected from zoos and farms go to the lucrative art market. When engraved the shell reveals layers of colour from dark green through blue to white which creates a cameo effect.

smoked meat

Smoking emu meat is an excellent long-term storage method that brings out the subtle flavour of the bird. Several 'drum' sections are suitable for smoking and may be smoked in one large piece to retain the oils and fats stored in the sinews. The fat will

4 Wheeler/Warwick Kent

Packaged emu meat, a product of Western Australia.

4 Wheeler/Warwick Kent

Smoked emu drum, a product of Western Australia, smoked in Victoria by Yarra Valley venison.

condition a prosciutto-style of emu meat, promoting maximum moisture retention from the drying effects of smoke. Smoke can rob the meat of up to 30 per cent of its moisture and volume, placing the already expensive meat in the luxury bracket.

In 1990, Swiss charcutier Vincent Muster experimented with the smoking technique. He found that rubbing a combination of crushed dried leaves of lemon-scented myrtle (*Backhousia citriodora*) and Tasmanian mountain pepper (*Tasmannia lanceolata*), onto the surface of the meat prior to smoking produced the serendipity of seasonings. This native spice rub is now generally accepted by many exponents of Australian cuisine as the perfect seasoning for emu meat.

Smoking emu meat became popular when the serving of rare emu fan fillets to restaurant diners proved difficult. Diners believed they were being served rare beef and, when told that this 'beef' was emu, were horrified at the thought of eating under-done poultry. They had of course expected the emu (being poultry) to have a white flesh. This embarrassing occurrence meant that the serving strategy for emu had to be rethought. When emu meat was reintroduced at Riberries as a prosciutto, it received rave compliments. The consumer learnt that emu, being a red meat, is technically game and needs to be served rare.

'ema'

In 1696 on the west coast of Australia the Dutch explorer Willem de Vlamingh found the footprints of a large bird thought to be an 'ema'. *Ema* was the Portuguese word for the long-legged crane of the Old World. The name was applied to all ostrich-like birds discovered in the New World.

The first sighting by an English colonist was in 1788 near the present site of Sydney's Central Railway Station. The bird was shot by a convict under the instruction of Governor Phillip and, on close scrutiny, it was decided that it should be called the 'New South Wales emu'. Today the word 'emu' is used exclusively for the Australian bird.

<sizzled 'ema' and port>

SERVES 4

- 2 emu fan fillets
- 3 tablespoons olive oil for the marinade and cooking
- Dorrigo pepperleaf or milled black pepper
- 4 oranges, juiced and strained (reserving the rind of 2 of the oranges in thin strips)
- 1 nip (30 ml / 1 fl oz) Grand Marnier or similar
- port (equal quantity of port to orange juice)
- salt to season

1. Marinate the fan fillets in the oil and pepper for 1 to 2 hours.
2. Heat a skillet on top of a hot flame for a good 5 minutes.
3. Place the fan fillets straight from the oil marinade into the skillet.
4. Cook for 7 to 8 minutes, turning the fillets to cook both sides.
5. Remove the fillets from the skillet and keep them warm under a tea towel.
6. Add the rind to the skillet and fry off a little. Then add the liqueur and stir.
7. Add the orange juice and port and reduce to one third.
8. Bring the fillets back to the pan and add a little salt.
9. Keep turning the meat while the sauce continues to reduce to a glaze.
10. Remove the fillets and let them stand for 5 minutes. (This is standard practice with all game and, indeed, all roasts.)
11. Slice across the grain.

<carpaccio-style emu>

Carpaccio is a raw meat cured by means of salt and air drying. Marcel Bouvier recommends drum fillets for this recipe.

1 kg (2 lb) emu

40 g (1½ oz) coarse sea salt

1 tablespoon roughly chopped pepperberries

2 lemon-scented myrtle leaves

150 ml (5 fl oz) brandy

1. Trim emu meat of any sinews and wipe dry.
2. Rub the salt, pepperberries and leaves into the meat and store in a container in the refrigerator for a week, turning it every 24 hours.
3. Remove the meat from the container. Discard the juices.
4. Put a cake rack inside a clean container, place the meat on the cake rack and put another cake rack on top of the meat (so that the meat is sandwiched between the two racks). Put a heavy weight on top of the uppermost rack. Refrigerate and leave the meat for a week. Discard the juices.
5. Place the cured meat in a wire-mesh fish griller and allow it to dry in a well-ventilated, fly-screened area for a minimum of 10 days.

<smoked emu>

The smoke is created using sawdust. Do not use pine sawdust as it imparts a bitter flavour. The hairs rubbed off banksia cones and soaked are a good alternative to sawdust and give the emu that genuine Australian flavour. Use a large kettle oven if a smokehouse is not available.

1 kg (2 lb) mid or outside emu drum

2 g coarse sea salt

1 tablespoon roughly chopped pepperberries

2 lemon-scented myrtle leaves

150 ml (5 fl oz) brandy

1. Trim emu meat of any sinews and wipe dry.
2. Rub the salt, pepperberries and leaves into the meat and place in a container in the refrigerator for a week, turning it every 24 hours.
3. Remove the meat from the container. Discard the juices.
4. Hang the meat in a smokehouse for 3 hours on a very low heat. If a smokehouse is not available, place the meat in a preheated kettle oven for 3 hours (use only 6 to 8 heat beads) with the top and bottom vents both open.
5. Serve thinly sliced.

Note: Smoked emu can be stored for several weeks wrapped in a clean, cotton cloth (do not wrap in plastic). Serve with Pickled Billy-goat Plums (recipe, page 198).

4 Wheeler/Warwick Kent

Smoked emu salad presented on Xanthorrhoea, a grass tree.

<emu liver pâté>

500 g (16 oz) emu liver
150 ml (5 fl oz) brandy
20 g (⅔ oz) salt
2 bay leaves
4 sassafras leaves
1 large onion, chopped
500 g (16 oz) pork fat
2 eggs
50 g (2 oz) plain flour (all-purpose flour)
clean sheets of paperbark for lining the terrine

Marcel Bouvier's emu liver pâté is famous. The following recipe is a household version adapted from the commercially-produced pâté. Marcel Bouvier runs the very popular Beecroft Butchery–Charcuterie in Beecroft, Sydney.

1. Clean the emu livers and chop them into small pieces.
2. Marinate the liver for 2 days in the brandy, salt, leaves and chopped onion. Stir a few times.
3. Remove the leaves and the liver from the marinade. Discard the leaves.
4. Put the liver and the pork fat into a food processor. Mince them together very finely.
5. Beat the eggs and add them to the mince along with the marinade, flour and salt.
6. Line the terrine with paperbark, cutting it to fit.
7. Pour in the mixture.
8. Cover the pâté with another sheet of paperbark.
9. Place the terrine in a tray that has 4 cm (1½ in) of hot water, and cook in an oven (preheated to 160°C / 325°F)for 1½ to 2 hours.
10. Allow the terrine to cool. Put it in the refrigerator for 36 hours to set.

Warwick Kent

Coarse emu liver pâté wrapped and baked in paperbark, served with pumpkin melba toast.

Barramundi

< *lates calcarifer* >

The barramundi is an ancient fish. It belongs to the family of giant perch that swam rivers and estuaries in the Eocene epoch 55 million years ago. Today it lives in the brackish rivers, creeks and swamps of lush tropical and sub-tropical northern Australia. There are several varieties of *lates calcarifer*. Barramundi found in estuaries or areas of higher salinity tend to be elongated with a green-grey upper body and a silver lower body with yellowish fins. Freshwater barramundi have a much darker upper body and fins with a golden-coloured underbody and a much larger girth tapering into a strong thick tail.

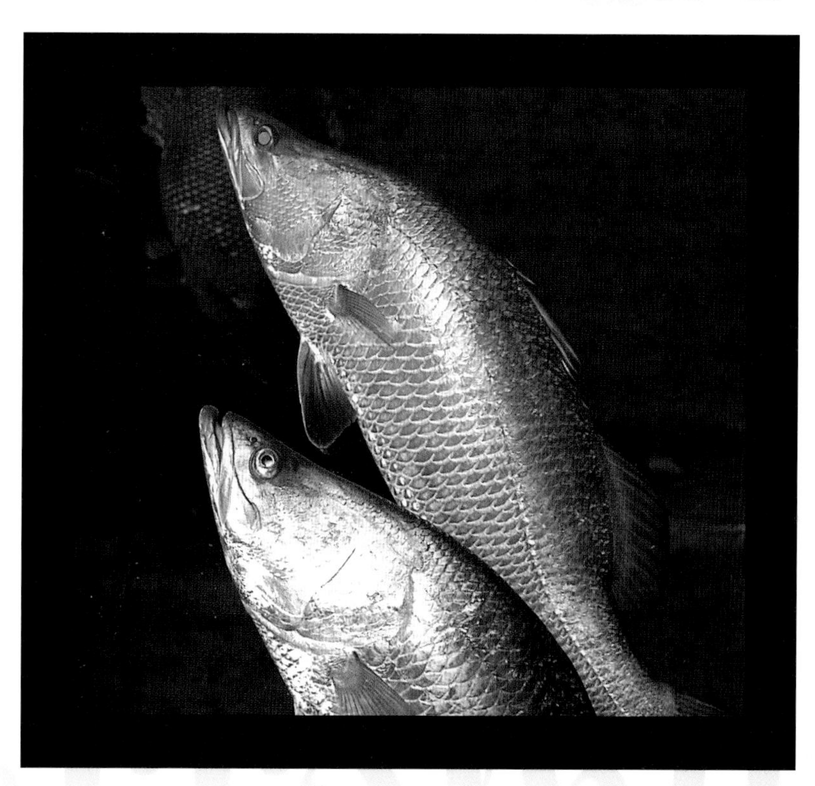

Barramundi is an Aboriginal word and is used for at least two other unrelated species bearing some resemblance to the giant perch — the large-scaled saratoga and the protected Queensland lungfish.

Another impersonator is the sand bass, or dwarf palmer, which is often referred to as the 'reef barramundi'. This fish grows to a maximum length of only 32 cm (13 in). Its dull brownish appearance gives it away as an impersonator.

following the seasons

Like the salmon, the barramundi is catadromous — it swims down river to the estuaries and coastal shallows to breed. In October and November (Dhuludur in the Arnhem Land calendar) the young barramundi journeys back upstream to mature in the upper-inland freshwater reaches.

In March and April (Mayaltha and Midawarra in the Arnhem Land calendar) the heavy rain and high spring tides inundate the grass-covered floodplains. Local Aborigines find this the ideal time for spearing barramundi. Barramundi can become caught in freshwater billabongs as the flood waters recede. These fish lay down heavy fatty deposits and acquire a darker colour — they are best grilled or baked. By mid-June (Dharratharr Mirra) the fish are found in plentiful numbers in any of the mangroves and creeks north of the Mary River in Queensland, right across to the north of the Ashburton River in central Western Australia.

transformer

Barramundi are protandrous hermaphrodites: the majority start life as males complete with functioning sexual organs, but eventually change to females. The sexual transformation occurs when the fish is four or five years old, during the wet-season months of January and February immediately after spawning. Over a period of eight weeks, the gonads disappear and are replaced by ovaries and tubular organs. A small percentage of barramundi do not complete the full male to female transition.

Very large specimens are almost exclusively female and live for up to 30 years, attaining a length of 1.5 metres (5 ft) and a weight of 55 kilograms (121 pounds). Female barramundi are easily the world's greatest egg carriers, producing close to 17 million eggs in one spawning. However, the flesh of these large specimens is not considered good eating.

The adult giant perch is a hungry carnivore and preys on crustaceans and smaller fish including its own offspring. Anglers generally aim for fish that are two to four years old and bait their hooks with live prawns, cherubins, small fish, frogs or large witjuti grubs.

preparation of the fish

Should one be fortunate enough to land a large 'barra', scaling the catch can be a challenge. The scales are large, round, flat, translucent discs about the size of a 20-cent piece (approximately

3 cm or 1¼ in in diameter). The scales fly off wildly when scraped and stick to surrounding surfaces.

Take care when handling barramundi as their sharp spines and razor-like gill covers can easily gash flesh. The third dorsal spine is the longest and strongest, but the smaller and not so obvious anal spines can be particularly dangerous. Generally, the bones of barramundi are some of the hardest found in fish and a hack-saw blade is recommended for cutting through them.

buyer beware

The *Lates calcarifer* is one of Australia's best eating fish. Sadly its reputation suffered throughout the 1970s and '80s because of substitution rorts, and the legacy of that malpractice is still felt in the 1990s.

The Nile perch (*Lates niloticus*), an imported African ocean perch and almost identical in appearance to *Lates calcarifer*, is occasionally sold as Australian barramundi by unscrupulous operators. This practice is highly illegal.

The fish available in Australian fish markets is usually a product of Queensland aquaculture. The 400 g (13 oz) baby barramundi are sometimes scaled, always gilled and gutted and then packed in ice. Some fish have their bones totally removed by a sophisticated machine which works like a sewing machine. A razor-sharp knife cuts along either side of spine and spinal barbs, removing them and the gut without breaking the soft belly. This impressive process allows the cook a choice of numerous culinary applications. The barramundi can be easily stuffed or simply turned inside-out for grilling or pan frying.

cooking methods

Barramundi is a very fine eating fish and should be cooked gently on medium heat. A high-temperature barbecue will sometimes crisp the outside of the fish and give it an uncharacteristically strong taste.

Donald Thomson. Courtesy of Mrs Dorita Thomson and Museum of Victoria.

Fish trapping, circa 1935.

fish traps

Spearing, netting, line fishing and stupefying are all common indigenous fishing methods, but the exploitation of seasonal fish movements and water level changes is perhaps the most technical and effective method practised by Aborigines.

Toward the end of the wet season, when receding waters cause estuarine fish to move back downstream, hunters would construct a weir with a funnelled opening across the stream. The weir had to be strong enough to raise water levels by about one metre (40 inches), with overflows on either bank to relieve the mounting pressure. Stringbark was used to make a spout large enough to carry the fish through and a grass matting layer below the spout ensured that all fish were captured.

The indigenous way of cooking barramundi is by far the best and easiest method with no need for scaling or cutting through the bones. The whole fish is gutted and cooked in a shallow pit oven which has been dug in the sand. Specially-collected flat stones, are heated in the pit on top of a hot fire. When the fire has subsided, green grass and fresh leaves are placed over the stones. The fish is wrapped in paperbark, placed in the pit, and some of the hot rocks are laid over the parcel. The pit is loosely filled with sand and the fish is left to cook.

Warwick Kent

Whole barramundi wrapped in paperbark and cooked in a ground oven.

<barramundi in paperbark>

Prepare a cooking pit as described earlier in this chapter. Light a fire in a trough 40 cm (16 in) deep in the sand using a mixture of small and large chunks of wood to create even coals. A pit made in sand allows the heat and steam to travel effectively. Clay soil will trap all the heat and steam creating a hotter oven. Hard wood will give even heat. If you can't use a cooking pit, use a large, fan-forced oven.

1. Wash the barramundi under a hose.
2. Make a blanket using several rolls of paperbark or a large sheet of bark and place the whole barramundi in its centre. Add aromatics if desired. Fold edges over the fish and secure tightly with butcher's twine.
3. Place the fish into the pit or into a large, fan-forced oven.
4. Fish in pit: cooking time varies between 1 and 1½ hours. Let the fish stand for 15 minutes before unwrapping.
5. Fish in oven: cook for 1 hour at 200°C (400°F). Let the fish stand for 15 minutes before unwrapping.
6. Use poultry scissors or secateurs to cut through the string and paperbark.

1 large whole barramundi

enough paperbark to wrap the whole fish

aromatics such as lemon-scented myrtle, Dorrigo pepper, Tasmanian mountain pepper or thyme (optional)

at least 5 m (16 ft) of butcher's twine

<baby barramundi in mirin>

ALLOW 1 FISH PER PERSON

- 1 whole baby barramundi per person
- mirin (Japanese sweet rice wine)
- green ginger, finely grated
- cornflour (cornstarch)
- salt and pepper to season
- oil for frying
- a lime or lemon for serving
- teriyaki sauce for serving

In this recipe, the fish skeleton is cooked separately to set its shape. It can then be used as a frame for the presentation of the fish.

1. Wash the fish and remove any loose scales.
2. Fillet both sides with a sharp knife, leaving the tail on the skeleton. Reserve the skeleton.
3. Cut each fillet diagonally into 3 pieces.
4. Marinate the fish pieces in the mirin and ginger for 15 to 20 minutes.
5. Skewer the fish skeleton by piercing it from the tail through to the head with a long bamboo skewer. This will give the fish a slightly bowed effect. Flour generously and shake off excess.
6. If possible, cook the fish skeleton just above a barbecue of dying hot coals. Alternatively, bake the skeleton in a medium oven at 200°C (400°F) for approximately 15 minutes, or until golden.
7. Remove the fish pieces from the marinade and place on a wire rack to dry.
8. Season the fish and dust it with cornflour. Shake off any excess.
9. Heat some oil in a wok and deep fry the pieces until they are golden brown (approximately 3 minutes).
10. Drain the pieces well, then place them back onto the cooked skeleton.
11. Serve with fresh lime or lemon and a small vessel of teriyaki sauce.

<barrabroth>

SERVES 6 – 8

- barramundi head and wings
- 3 sticks celery, cut to chunks
- 3 sassafras leaves
- 1 onion, quartered
- 1 teaspoon whole white peppercorns
- 1 to 2 sprigs of tarragon
- shredded coriander leaf for garnish
- light soy sauce for serving

1. Put the head, wings, celery, sassafras leaves, onion, pepper and tarragon into a tall stock-pot. Add enough water to cover 3 cm (1 in) above fish.
2. Simmer for 1 hour over a medium heat. Do not boil.
3. Turn off heat and allow to stand for 15 minutes.
4. Ladle the stock into a muslin-lined strainer, leaving the last two ladlefuls behind.
5. Remove the cheeks from the barra head and the long white muscle meat from the wings and add them to the hot broth.
6. Serve with shredded coriander leaf and a hint of light soy sauce.

Warwick Kent

Baby barramundi in mirin prepared in the style of Voshikazu Tsuji of Tsujitome Restaurant, Tokyo, Japan.

<blackened barra cutlet>

SERVES 4

1 teaspoon ground black pepper
1 teaspoon cayenne pepper
1 teaspoon white pepper
½ teaspoon thyme
½ teaspoon oregano
½ teaspoon garlic powder
½ teaspoon onion and chilli powder
½ teaspoon chilli powder
4 barramundi cutlets
300 g (10 oz) butter, melted

Cajun and creole cuisine emerged from the mysterious swamplands of Louisiana which were settled in the 18th century by the French-speaking people of Acadia, the marine province of Canada. These people were deported to this region, having been forced by the British to leave their homeland. Cajun cuisine uses spices from the West Indies, hot peppers from Spain and African okras which all grew well in the fertile swamp of the Bayou. This recipe requires a very hot plate to seal the spices. It is best cooked outside as it produces a fair amount of smoke.

1. Mix all the herbs and spices together.
2. Pat dry the fish cutlets.
3. Coat one side of the fish with melted butter.
4. Shake the herbs and spices over the coated side of the fish.
5. Wait until the butter has set the herbs and spices to the flesh.
6. Cook the seasoned side for 1½ to 2 minutes.
7. Turn the fish over to cook the other side. Do not return to the blackened side. The longer this side is cooked, the stronger the flavour will be.

Note: Over the years I have worked at reproducing the Cajun concept of blackening fish using native aromatics. Today my blend is available pre-mixed. So in place of the herbs and spices listed in the ingredients, you can substitute one jar of Gundabluey 'Blackened Fish Blend'.

Warwick Kent

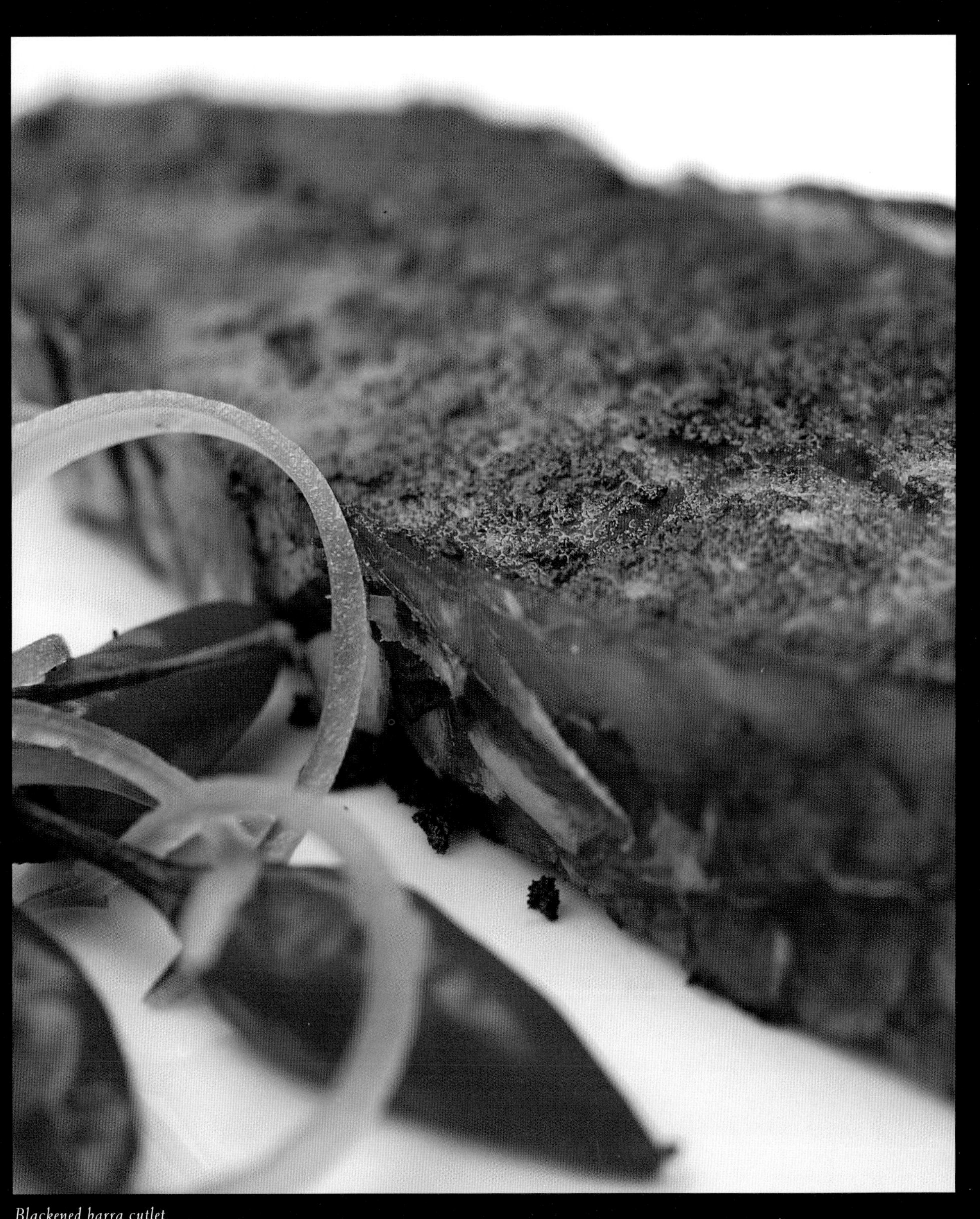

Blackened barra cutlet.

Magpie goose & cape barren goose

< *Anseranas semipalmata* and *Cereopsis novaehollandiae* >

In Australia there are two birds of considerable interest among the wild geese population: the magpie goose and the Cape Barren goose. Maligned by agriculturalists and pastoralists and an easy target for shooters these geese have suffered a grave decline since white settlement. A recent strategy of close conservation management and commercial farming of native geese, although in its infancy, will ensure their survival, making them part of the sustainable bush-food industry. Despite gradual increases in wild geese numbers in their natural habitat, these birds have a long way to go to regain their former prominence.

three geese, one nest

The geese travel as a family unit of one male with one or two females within a flock of up to 1000 birds. A flock is not stable and families move freely between other flocks.

During the Arnhem Land season of 'Midawarr' (in April) the geese lay an average of eight creamy-white eggs, which soon become nest-stained. Hatching will occur after 24 days. The young birds must be ready to fly at 11 weeks in order to avoid the encroaching dry season and the rapidly diminishing food source.

the magpie goose

The magpie goose (*Anseranas semipalmata*) is the sole species member within one genus. The name of the genus itself is a combination of the Latin for 'goose' (*anser*) and 'duck' (*anas*) because the bird is neither one nor the other.

This black and white waterfowl has goose-like habits and a swan-like appearance and is between a duck and a black swan in size. Its posture makes it unmistakable — its long neck allows it to feed in swamps and see over tall reeds and assists in building its complex nest. The bird has long legs to wade through deep water, preferring to walk rather than swim. The magpie goose has partially-webbed feet — hence its name *semipalmated* — and has large claws. In the course of its wandering, the bird will cover a great distance over dry hard ground. It often roosts in trees. As a safety measure against the dangers of the swamp the magpie goose successively moults its primary flight feathers and is therefore never flightless — although its flight is laboured.

HOW TO COOK YOUR MAGPIE GOOSE

Colonial cookbooks and more contemporary recipes have demonstrated little imagination in cooking native wildfowl, usually only considering roasting and broiling. It can be like a lottery trying to cook wild magpie geese as the age and condition of the bird will be unknown quantities. The only way to determine the true cooking requirements for a recipe is by using a farmed goose. A farmed magpie goose weighs around two kilograms (four pounds) and has thick, dark-red breast meat that looks strikingly similar to venison. The legs and thighs are small compared with the size of breast and, unlike turkey, are not laced with strong muscle sinews.

Warwick Kent

Dressed magpie geese on scales.

Colonial cookbooks recommend roasting wildfowl until it is well done. This is definitely not advised for the magpie goose. Baking and continually basting in a moderate oven for only 55 minutes gives a juicy, plump result. Looks, however, are deceptive. The breasts are greyed, juiceless and tough with a nondescript flavour. The thighs cook well but the drumsticks, being small, shrivel and become wasted. Roasting is definitely not the best way to cook this goose.

in the arafura swamp, 1937

Magpie geese and their eggs are an important traditional food for Aborigines in the north, where ancestral hunting rights are practised. In the Daly River area the eggs are associated with fertility and seasonal increase. The goose is known to the Top End people by a variety of names, including ***gurrmattji, kuramutchi, muldrie*** **and** ***newalgang*****.**

Traditional magpie-goose hunting is best recorded in the writings of Donald F. Thomson, who lived and worked among the people of north-east Arnhem Land during the 1930s. His journals and photographs record a hunt in the Arafura Swamp in the wet season of 1937 when the mosquitoes were abundant and persistent and the leeches plentiful.

Donald Thomson. Courtesy of Mrs Dorita Thomson and Museum of Victoria

Polling through the Arafura Swamp in nardan canoes, hunting magpie geese.

Thomson describes the beehive-shaped communal paperbark houses with entrances that could be blocked with grass that the goose hunters built to get some respite from the attacking insects. At times when they were hunting geese at a great distance from the communal shelter the men would build platforms in trees above the swamp. The upper-most branches of the tree would be broken down to replenish the smoking fire that rested on mud-covered paperbark sheets on the platform. The smoke offered only minor protection, however, from the plague of mosquitoes. With sleep near impossible, the men would huddle around the fire and beat themselves with fans made from magpie goose wings.

Goose hunting and egg collection in the swamps was carried out in specially-constructed stringbark canoes called ***nardans*****. The stringbark was smoked to prevent cracking or splitting, then shaped, stitched and caulked. These fragile canoes were propelled through the swamps with the aid of a pole and rarely lasted longer than two trips. Roasted eggs and cooked geese were the reward. When the hunters returned to camp, the women would feast on goose while the men, now tired of their goose diet, satisfied their craving for vegetable foods.**

A far superior and more practical method is to sear and pan-fry the individual legs, thighs and breast sections. Searing in a hot skillet with a little oil and seasoning followed by a lengthy rest period in a warm environment produces juicy and full-flavoured meat. Breast meat requires searing for only a short time and is best served medium rare. The boned thighs and drumsticks, being muscle meat, benefit from longer exposure to heat. The flavour of the leg meat is quite different from that of the breast and is comparable to duck meat. The neck and carcass make a reasonable broth.

As the magpie goose is a game bird, the fresh product is always best. Freezing and thawing the breast meat means that water will be lost in the thawing, the meat will cook more quickly and you will lose the edge in taste and texture.

The tender venison-like flesh of the breast tastes superb and does not require the adulteration of heavy sauces. You can confidently serve the meat sauceless with a plate of ribbon yam chips.

hunting today

Very strict hunting regulations are in place and there are substantial fines for not observing them. Up to seven wild geese can be taken by each hunter in any one day, but no hunter can have more than 21 geese in his or her possession at one time. All geese shot must be for personal consumption as no sale, barter or exchange of waterfowl is allowed. At the end of the hunting season the

Nature Focus Library/I.J. Skira

Cape Barren geese (Cereoposis novaehollandiae).

hunter should not have more than 21 geese in the freezer.

he cape barren goose

The Cape Barren goose (*Cereopsis novaehollandiae*), like the magpie goose, does not fit easily into the true 'goose' category. The Cape Barren goose is the sole living representative of the genus *Cereopsis*.

This ash-grey grazing bird is skeletally similar to true geese and shelducks. Although it has a distinctive appearance, the species has in the past been confused with and likened to swans.

Cape Barren geese favour grassy areas, beaches and rocky prominences. They breed in the grassy scrub on the Furneaux Group in Bass Strait, where they were known by the indigenous people as *toolka*. They are also found on the islands off Wilson's Promontory, Victoria, the islands of Spencer Gulf, South Australia and the Recherche Archipelago, Western Australia.

Cape Barren geese are thought to mate for life and are found in pairs throughout the year.

FARMING THE CAPE BARREN GOOSE

For those brought up on the flavour of Cape Barren goose, and for those who would like to sample it, the bird lends itself well to commercial farming.

The economic downturn in the wool industry prompted Chris Rhodes of Flinders Island to propose the farming of Cape Barren geese. In October 1995, with the approval of the Tasmanian Department of Parks, Wildlife and Heritage, a Code of Practice for the Welfare of Animals was drafted relating to the husbandry systems and welfare of farmed Cape Barren geese.

Birds have been selectively harvested from the wild to form the basis of a breeding stock which, it is hoped, will be self-replacing within three years of production. To keep stress levels to a minimum, the geese are maintained on pastures that accommodate their territorial and aggressive behaviour — approximately four or five breeding pairs for each hectare (two-and-a-half acres).

Not only does commercial farming appear to be the saviour of the Cape Barren goose, it also preserves a traditional food source and returns it to the appreciative diner.

nesting

The time of nest building varies according to climatic conditions. Nesting occurs from May to July and will be delayed if the summer and autumn are dry. The clutch of elliptical, glossy-white, coarsely-textured eggs each measure about 8.3 cm (3¼ in) in length. The number of eggs laid ranges between one and seven, but the average is four. The incubation period is 35 days and goslings hatch from July to mid August. At the end of the breeding season the adult bird moults and is rendered flightless until spring. Cape Barren geese will abandon their eggs if disturbed, however they can produce a replacement clutch. Nature's second chance allows the commercial farmer to selectively collect eggs for artificial incubation, substantially increasing the reproductive rate of the farmed flock.

<confit of goose legs>

- 1 goose drumstick and 1 thigh per serve, separated at the joint with the skin removed
- ½ teaspoon cumin seeds
- ½ teaspoon coriander seeds
- zest of 1 lime, free of pith, cut into thin strips
- ¼ teaspoon salt
- 500 g (16 oz) coconut butter

This dish is suitable for yum cha.

1. Blend the dry ingredients and rub into the skinless pieces of goose.
2. Place the pieces into a bowl. Cover and refrigerate for 48 hours.
3. Melt the coconut butter and pour it into a medium-sized earthenware pot with high sides and a lid.
4. Pat dry the goose legs and thighs and drop the pieces into the coconut butter.
5. Cook on stove top over low heat for 30 minutes.
6. Place in oven at 170°C (340°F) and cook for a further 2 ½ hours.
7. Let cool overnight before placing in the refrigerator, ready for use.

<goose broth with lemon-scented myrtle>

MAKES 1000 – 1200 MLS

Magpie and Cape Barren geese are expensive game birds to purchase. The breast and leg meat comprise 70 per cent of the carcass weight. The long necks and the body are very flavoursome when used in stocks and broths.

1. Fry the carcass in a large frying pan with a little olive oil until brown.
2. Place the carcass in a tall stockpot and add the remaining ingredients except for the salt.
3. Bring slowly to the boil (but do not boil).
4. Simmer to reduce liquid by one-third.
5. Turn off the heat and let stand for 10 minutes.
6. Ladle out into a strainer lined with muslin cloth or filter paper.
7. Reheat the strained broth almost to boiling point. Season with salt.
8. Serve in miso cups with a shredded lemon-scented myrtle leaf per cup.

goose carcass (feet, legs, necks and rib section)

olive oil

1 large onion studded with 2 bay leaves and four cloves

1 large carrot, sliced

2 celery sticks, no leaves

1 tablespoon whole black peppercorns

6 lemon-scented myrtle leaves, fresh or dried

2 litres water

salt to taste

Warwick Kent

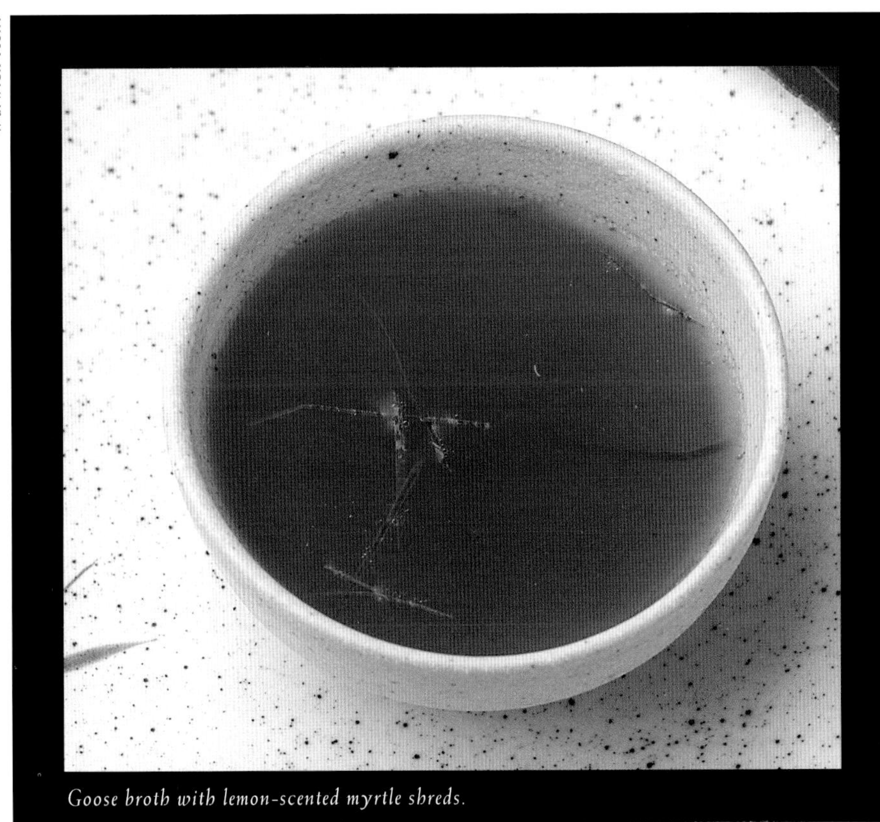

Goose broth with lemon-scented myrtle shreds.

<seared goose breasts>

SERVES 4

- 1 magpie goose or Cape Barren goose, preferably fresh
- salt and white pepper
- 150 ml (5 fl oz) olive oil
- ½ teaspoon sesame oil

Delicious with quandongs or with Warm Salad (recipe, next page).

1. Remove the legs (reserve them for Confit of Goose Legs, page 94). Carefully ease the breast meat off the rib cage using a sharp fillet knife.
2. Rub salt and pepper onto the breast skin and flesh.
3. Heat a heavy-based pan, pour in oils and sear the breast for 7 minutes on the skin side and 4 minutes on the other side.
4. Let breasts stand for 8 to 10 minutes before slicing.

Warwick Kent

Seared magpie goose breasts.

<warm salad>

SERVES 4

1. Core and flatten capsicums. Remove the ribs. Divide the capsicums into wide strips and cut into triangular shapes.
2. Wok-fry prepared capsicums with the ginger, garlic and chilli. Keep aside.
3. Arrange the leaves on a warmed plate.
4. Scatter the warm capsicum mixture over the leaves, and drizzle over some of the dressing.
5. Place thinly sliced goose meat over the salad, adding more dressing if required. Sprinkle with freshly-diced red capsicum.

1 each small red, green and yellow capsicums (bell peppers) plus extra red capsicum for sprinkling

1 tablespoon thinly-sliced fresh ginger, cut into fine strips

2 cloves garlic, very finely chopped

½ teaspoon finely-chopped chilli

leaves of butter lettuce, washed and towel-dried

leaves of coral lettuce, washed and towel-dried

leaves of winter tarragon (aniseed grass or *tageta alucida*)

seared goose breast

THE DRESSING

Combine the following ingredients:

½ cup (125 ml / 4 fl oz) virgin olive oil

1 tablespoon sweet soy sauce

½ teaspoon ground coriander seeds

½ tablespoon balsamic vinegar

½ teaspoon sesame oil

pinch of salt

barks & fuels

Australian Aborigines use specific barks, woods, cones and leaves for particular purposes. Barks are used for cooking and other food-related activities, also for shelter, canoes, poisons, medicines and sometimes aphrodisiacs. A variety of wood, cones and leaves are used as fuels for cooking.

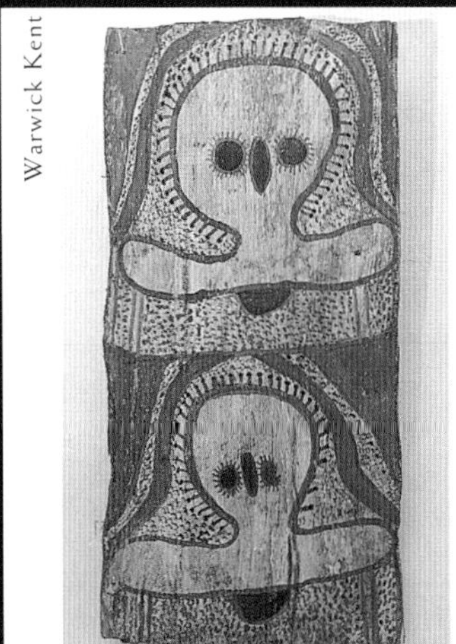

'Wanjina, the Water Spirit', bark painting from the Kimberley region, artist unknown.

Today bark art provides a number of communities with an income and international appreciation. The subjects of bark painting are often closely related to the rock art of a particular region. In the Kimberleys, for example, the Wandjinas — powerful creative beings of the Dreaming who directly control and influence the patterns of weather — are a traditional subject. Contemporary bark art of the Northern Territory portrays traditional foods, often in elaborate x-ray designs, revealing the importance of particular sections of the subject.

101 uses for paperbark

The most versatile and adaptable of barks is paperbark, which belongs to the genus *Melaleuca*, many different species of which are found throughout Australia. Paperbark is composed of cork cells sandwiched between thin sheets of papery bark — the thickness varies considerably among the species.

Paperbark has a variety of uses: containers made of paperbark provide an easy means of transporting food and water; some aborigines made temporary huts, humpies or *gunyahs* from large sheets of waxy paperbark found near swamps. In areas where paperbarks were scarce, the more rigid ironbark was substituted. In Central Australia, paperbark torches and flares were used for night walks, and firesticks made from the bark of a similar tree were used for burning back grasslands.

Aborigines in Arnhem Land used a crude paperbark glove for protection while handling the toxic djanga plant or moving hot stones when preparing a cooking pit. Ceremonial bread made from detoxified macrozamia seeds was wrapped in paperbark and baked in hot ashes. In the Daly River area, south west of Darwin, Aborigines preserve shark meat by tightly wrapping the flesh with leaves in paperbark to squeeze out all the moisture. On Groote Eylandt in the Gulf of Carpentaria women used paperbark as a modesty screen for hiding from the view of men while in public.

cooking with paperbark

Paperbark is a useful, renewable and recyclable resource. In some areas of food preparation, it is much better to use paperbark than aluminium foil. Wrapping and cooking potatoes in wet paperbark in an open fire, or in a domestic oven, guarantees a superb vegetable with a moist, full-flavoured centre.

Using paperbark as an insulator to cook fish, especially salmon and trout, gives a perfectly moist result because the fish does not cook too quickly. The stored heat within the bark parcel completes the cooking process away from the heat source.

Kenneth Leung, chef at The Watermark Restaurant at Balmoral Beach in Sydney, bakes oysters under a sheet of paperbark. The result is lightly cooked oysters with a subtle 'mushroom-smoked' flavour that leaves a very pleasant after-taste on the palate.

Damper wrapped in paperbark and baked gives the outer crust of the bush bread an interesting texture and colour it amazing shades of gold, beige, maroon and brown.

fuels

Good fuels are essential in the art of baking bush dampers. Quinine bush (*Alstonia constricta*) is reputably among the best. A common species of softwood scrub that exudes a milky latex when broken, this sub-coastal tree of New South

Wales and Queensland was named 'bitter bark' by Baron von Mueller because of its extremely bitter taste.

Gidgee (*Acacia cambagei*), one of the world's hardest and heaviest woods is another good fuel for outdoor cooking. This tree is found inland and is well known for its strong and somewhat offensive odour. Gidgee produces an intense heat and is highly regarded as a firewood.

Belah (*Casuarina cristata*) is a very hard wood and another preferred fuel. The tree is widely distributed inland and grows generally in heavy soils.

Oil-rich trees, such as kerosene wood (*Halfordia kendack*), will burn green as will the bastard sandalwood (*Eremophila mitchelii*) also known as the budda tree. These trees burn well and do not taint foods cooked in their fires.

Fuels to be avoided are the dogwood (*Jacksonia scoparia*) of the east coast and the leopardwood (*Flindersia maculosa*) of the dry inland, both of which give meat a very unpleasant flavour.

Banksia cones and eucalyptus leaves thrown on the fire or placed in the oven will impart their smoky flavour to food.

Paperbark, used as a jacket for poultry cooked in a convection kettle oven, will effectively permeate the meat with a smoky mushroom flavour. A kettle oven creates similar cooking conditions to those of a ground oven that has been scooped out in the shape of a shallow dish. Sheets of paperbark laid across the food in the ground oven are vital to the result of the cooked fare, as no smoke must escape nor sand enter. Paperbark and fragrant fuels are part and parcel of good cooking.

coolamons

Warwick Kent

Assorted coolamons with banksia.

Coolamons are important tools made by women for their personal use. Men seldom use these implements. Coolamons used for gathering and carrying honey, fruits, nuts and berries are generally made from wood. A paperbark carrier is similar to a coolamon — it is simply a sheet of bark with the ends gathered and tied with vines. Wooden coolamons are used as tools for digging for roots, tubers and water.

Hollow sections of living trees are used for a strong, rigid and long-lasting utensil. The women work in pairs and use one of two methods: they either mark the shape of the coolamon onto the curve of the tree trunk and then use a sharp stone to excise the wood; or they hollow out a large section of tree root. The rough shape is worked back to the sapwood with a stone adze, after which the coolamon is set in a hot bed of ashes. Sticks are wedged across the opening of the coolamon to prevent it from curling closed while drying.

Coolamons have different names depending on their particular use: *piti* is the Pitjantjatjara word for a coolamon used as a water vessel; *kanilpa* is a wider coolamon used for winnowing; and *wira* is a coolamon used as a scoop or shovel.

barks & fuels recipes

<smoking with banksia cones>

- 4 large fallen banksia cones with opened seed pods
- kettle-oven barbecue
- 60 heat beads (or the equivalent in charcoal fire-lighters, or a blow torch)
- meat or fish of your choice (see note)

One way to add the Australian flavour to meat or fish is to barbecue it in a kettle oven over braising coals with old-man banksia cones (*Banksia serrata*). This technique roasts the meat or fish while slightly smoking it. A kettle-oven barbecue brings a whole new dimension to barbecuing. Covered cooking has existed for many thousands of years in one form or another, always for the same reasons: to control the amount of oxygen available to the fire and to reduce the drying effect.

1. The day before you wish to barbecue, split each cone into 3 pieces and soak the pieces in water.
2. One hour before lighting the barbecue, drain the cones and dry them.
3. Light the barbecue with a fire lighter or by blow-torching the coals.
4. Wait until the coals or charcoal turn from glowing red to white.
5. Place the cones on top of the coals.
6. The fire is ready to use for cooking and will impart the flavour of the banksia. Make sure that the top and bottom vents of the kettle-oven barbecue are open.

Note: Using 60 beads, a 1.5 kg (3 lb) piece of meat will take 25 minutes to cook to medium rare. Leave to stand for 10 minutes before carving.

<tasmanian ocean trout baked in paperbark>

SERVES 12

1 x 2.5 kg (5½ lb) Tasmanian ocean trout, at room temperature, not direct from the refrigerator

1 roll of paperbark

thick-gauge butcher's twine

This fish is great with Lemon Aspen Mayonnaise (recipe, page 162) or Tomato and Muntrie Salsa (recipe, page 162).

Do not wash the fish for this recipe. A fresh trout should display quite a lot of mucilaginous substance over its body — this is the real sign that the fish is fresh.

1. Remove the trout's head, all body fins, the tail, belly flaps and pectoral wings. There is no need to scale the fish.
2. Unroll the paperbark, lay it flat and peel away any loose and torn layers.
3. Place the trout on the sheet. Fold one end of the bark over the head end of the trout and the other over the tail end. Roll the fish to enclose it completely in the paperbark. The skin of the fish will adhere to the paperbark, making scaling unnecessary – the bark becomes the natural serving apparel for the dish.
4. Tie a noose of butcher's twine tightly around the head part of the wrapped fish. Keep slipping nooses down the wrapped body of the trout and tighten — the same way as a butcher ties up a roast.
5. Place the wrapped fish in the oven at 200°C (400°F) for 19 minutes.
6. Remove the wrapped fish from the oven and let it stand for another 15 minutes in a warm, draught-free place.
7. Cut the twine with a pair of scissors, then cut the paperbark along the line of the trout's backbone and across the head and tail ends.
8. Gently split open the parcel by using your fingers to prise apart the two sides of the trout, keeping the paperbark in place. The flesh will lift from the bones, and the fish is ready to eat.

Note: The paperbark and skin can be composted.

Warwick Kent

Tasmanian ocean trout in paperbark with tomato and muntrie salsa.

< barbecued paperbark whirlygigs >

SERVES 6 – 8

sheet of paperbark

5 cups (800 g / 28 oz) of bunya nutmeal (see note)

2 cups (50 g / 2½ oz) tetragon, blanched, drained, squeezed and finely chopped

1 red capsicum (bell pepper), baked, skinned, seeded and cut into strips

butcher's twine

1. Lay the sheet of paperbark flat.
2. Place the cooked bunya nutmeal over one end of the paperbark, making a rectangle of 10 cm (4 in) by the width of the bark. Spread and flatten the meal out towards the edges of the rectangle. Press down firmly. The meal should be at least 2 cm (¾ in) thick.
3. Cover the bunya meal with a layer of tetragon, to a thickness of about 1–1½ cm (½–¾ in). Press down firmly.
4. Place the strips of prepared capsicum lengthways onto the filling.
5. Roll the paperbark, starting from the filled edge so that the capsicum is at the centre surrounded by the tetragon, which is surrounded by the bunya nutmeal and enclosed by the bark covering. Continue rolling until all the paperbark is used. Tie in place.
6. Place the parcel on the barbecue to heat through, and slice to serve.
7. Remove the paperbark before eating.

Note: The instructions for making bunya nutmeal are found in Step 1 of the pastry method for Tetragon and Mushroom Torte in Bunya (recipe, page 48).

< beer damper in paperbark >

SERVES 6 (1 IF VERY HUNGRY)

3 cups (500 g / 16 oz) self-raising flour

a good pinch of salt

375 ml (13 fl oz) beer (see note)

sheet of paperbark

butcher's twine

Some paperbark strands will adhere to the damper giving it a striking appearance. (Paperbark is non-toxic.)

1. Sift flour and salt into a bowl and make a well in the centre.
2. Pour warm beer into the centre and work the mixture from the centre to the sides.
3. Place the dough on top of a large sheet of paperbark and fold to cover.
4. Tie the parcel lightly to hold paperbark in place.
5. Bake in a preheated oven at 200°C (400°F) for 50 minutes.

Note: Cooper's Ale is very good for this recipe.

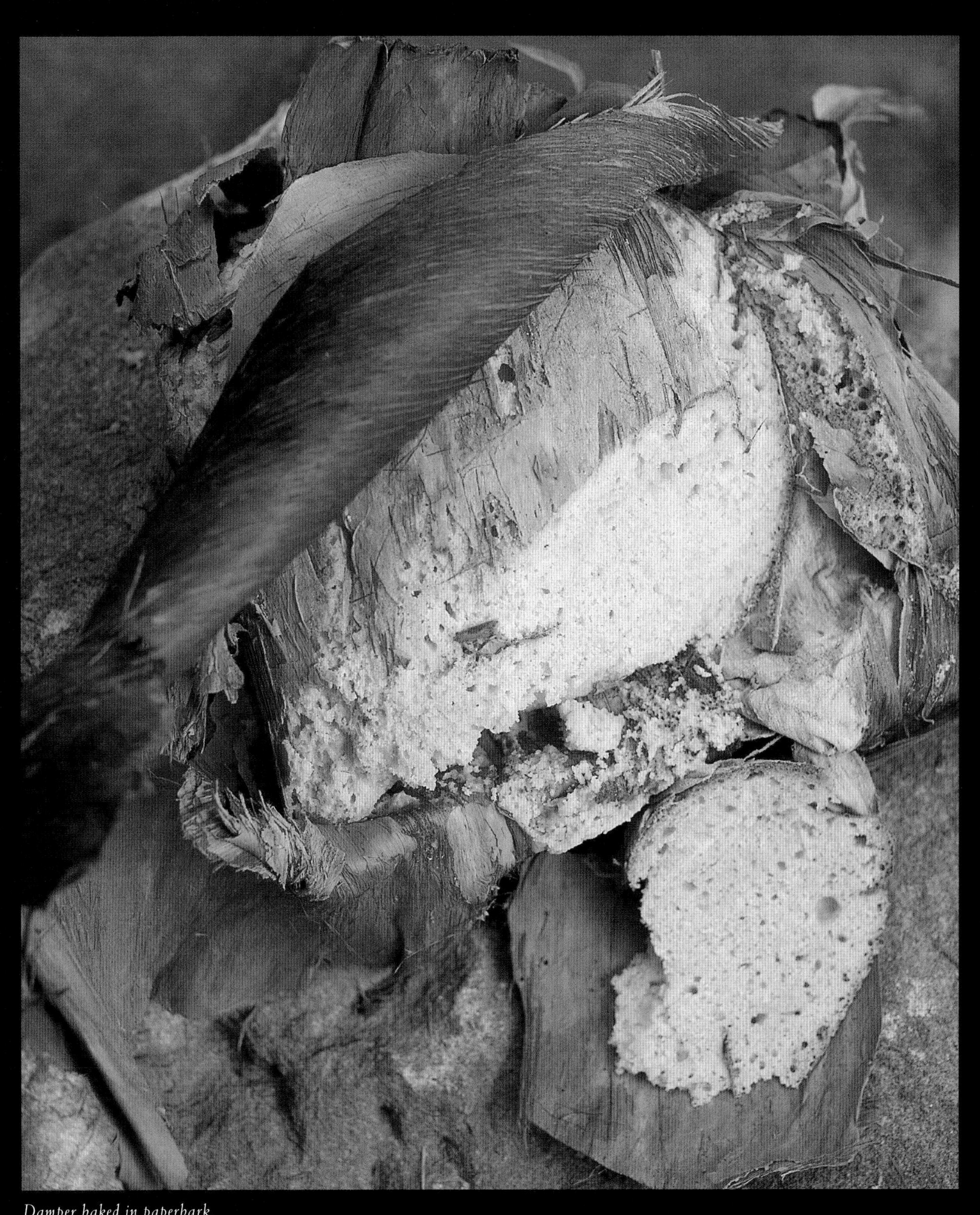
4 Wheeler/Warwick Kent

Damper baked in paperbark.

Sharks, skates & rays

< cartilaginous fish >

When the bounty of the ocean is considered, bony fish immediately come to mind. Lesser consideration is given to cartilaginous fish — fish that have a skeleton composed entirely of cartilage — the sharks, the skates and the rays.

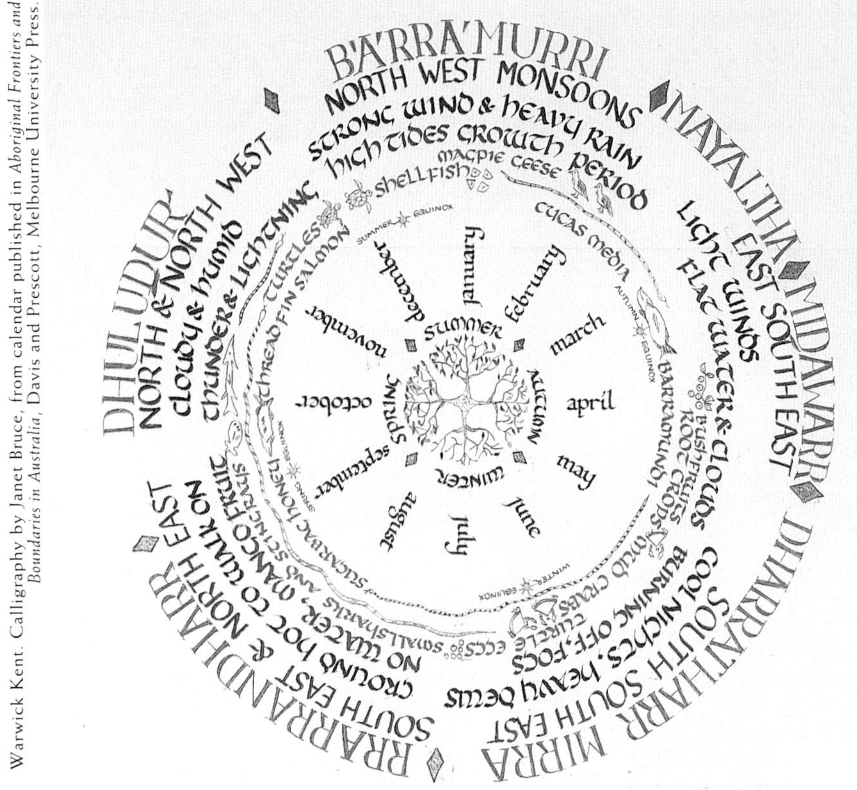

Warwick Kent. Calligraphy by Janet Bruce, from calendar published in *Aboriginal Frontiers and Boundaries in Australia*, Davis and Prescott, Melbourne University Press.

Bushfood calendar showing the seasons of Kakadu with weather conditions and variations outlined against the seasonal availability of foods.

It was cartilaginous fish, rather than bony fish, that attracted the attention of the early European explorers of Australia. Dampier named Shark Bay in Western Australia because of its astonishingly high number of sharks. The French expedition under the command of Baudin recorded sharing its catch of shark with the local tribe of Aborigines at Jervis Bay, New South Wales. On Sunday, 6 May 1770, while the *Endeavour* lay at anchor, Joseph Banks and James Cook dined on a meal of stingray served with the boiled leaves of tetragon. Of the stingray, Banks said: 'the fish itself was not quite so good as a skate nor was it much inferior, the tripe everybody thought excellent'. The ray weighed close to 136 kilograms (300 pounds).

Sharks, skates and rays have other distinguishing features that set them apart from bony fish. They have five to seven gill slits whereas bony fish have only one gill slit on each side. Their skeleton is lighter than bone, is firm, flexible, elastic and high in calcium and protein. Cartilaginous fish have tough skins. In place of scales, sharks have denticles (a material related to teeth); rays and skates have a partial covering of denticles.

sharks

There is an erroneous but popular belief that sharks are scavengers. In fact, they are very selective feeders. Having few predators, apart from humans, sharks are positioned right at the top of the marine food chain.

Sharks have been on the menu for years. The white boneless fillets from the 'fish and chip' shop are gummy shark, commonly called 'flake' and sometimes known as dog shark, dogfish or mango. This crustacean eater was popular with the Maoris of New Zealand, who would wash, gut and salt the shark before hanging it to dry for four to five months. The jerked flesh would be charred black over a good fire, then scraped to reveal a golden meat which was — perhaps because of its extremely strong smell — eaten in small helpings. In the Daly River area of the Northern Territory, shark meat was preserved by squeezing the flesh dry with absorbent paperbark. Shark fins have been used for making soup in China since ancient times, and have always been highly prized and highly priced.

rays and skates

Less selective than sharks in their diet are the rays. These ocean bottom dwellers have a preference for molluscs, crustaceans and other marine animals which bury themselves in sediment.

Rays and skates are large fish — the body discs of some species measure more than two m (six and a half ft) across and weigh as much as 350 kilograms (772 pounds). These cartilaginous fish fly through the water, propelled by a series of undulations down the pectoral fins, and trail a stinging whip-like barbed tail.

When Cook arrived at Botany Bay, stingrays were so abundant that 400 weight (about 900 kilograms, or 1985 pounds) were taken in one catch. From the drawings by Sydney Parkinson, the natural history artist of the *Endeavour* expedition, we know that the species captured was the smooth stingray (*Dasyatiis brevicaudatus*). This species, which Parkinson recorded as tasting similar to stewed turtle, is today referred to as Cook's stingray.

The sheer size of the rays must have been a challenge for John Thompson, the ship's one-handed cook, and his servant to prepare for the 84 men of the *Endeavour*.

The stingrays were taken in shallow water on a flowing tide. Cook noted that, although stingrays were easy to catch, the local Aborigines did not seem to partake of them. Cook saw evidence that the native people ate oysters, cockles, mussels and other fish, yet no remains of stingrays — not even barbs being used for weapon tips — were found around the camps.

Stingrays are, however, an important traditional food for the Aborigines of Northern Australia. The rays are caught from October to April, after the first thunderstorms of the wet season. If the liver is white-pink and oily, the ray is considered to be edible. The flesh and the liver are boiled or roasted separately and then minced together. The barbs are used for making spear tips. Manta rays and stingrays with two barbs are never eaten.

sweet and fresh

Odour is a vital and easy gauge of freshness. Ray and shark meats which are past their prime may take on a strong odour of ammonia. This is the result of the high quantity of urea maintained in the bloodstreams of these fish. Urea is necessary to balance the salt levels of the fish — the ammonia is released as the urea breaks down.

Stingray meat is white, sweet and firm and is generally sold as 'wings'. The wings should not be too large but — as an indicator of the peak of freshness — they should be well-coated with mucilage.

The small sharks sold through the fish markets as 'flake' are usually sold without heads. As with the ray, if the head and gut components are not removed soon after the catch, the strong smell of ammonia will quickly take over.

Flake should be very white at the head and have no smell at all. Any discolouration and hint of ammonia will instantly reveal that the fish was not processed quickly enough on board the fishing vessel.

PREPARATION OF THE FISH

The underside of a skate or ray is much thinner than the upper part and should be filleted first by running a flat knife along the cartilage. With the underside removed, the thicker upper side is much more manageable for filleting.

Skinning the ray or shark is done in the same way as any other fish. Use a hook or a dry towel to hold the tail end of the skin, cut straight down through the flesh to the skin, and turn the knife blade towards the top end of the fish. There is no need to saw with the knife — just shake the skin from side to side without moving the knife at all, and pull the tag of skin that you are holding secure. The skin will come away from the flesh easily.

DELICIOUS FISH

Ray and shark meat cook very well with wine, cider or vinegar — the possibilities are limitless!

Skate is regarded in England as a quality fish and fetches a good price. In Australia, however, skate, rays and sharks are still at the bottom of the price scale. As they are such good eating, the price is certain to move with the times.

A dish of stingray served with boiled tetragon leaves is the first recorded European meal eaten in this country — let's honour this gastronomic attempt and nationalise it as our own. It's a good one.

stingrays & botany

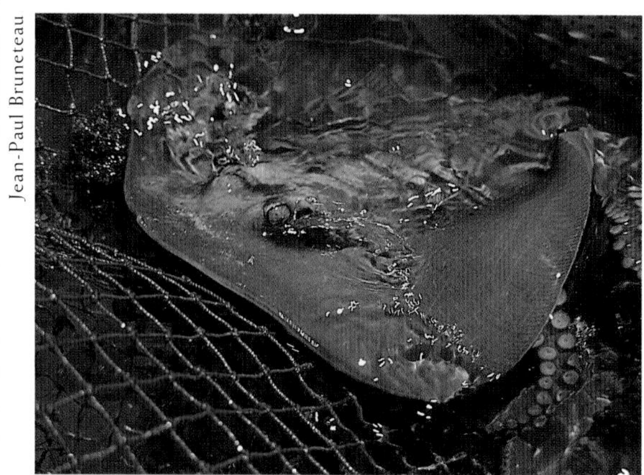

Jean-Paul Bruneteau

Small stingrays photographed at Kurnell, Botany Bay.

Sting-rays Harbour was the name Captain James Cook first gave to the bay in which he and his companions dined on stingray and tetragon. Cook subsequently decided to change the name to Botany Bay in honour of David Solander and Joseph Banks, who accompanied him on his voyage and who made invaluable contributions to the science of botany. The heads of the bay were named Cape Banks and Point Solander.

The *Endeavour* returned triumphantly to England with some 30 000 specimens collected on the voyage, 1600 of which were totally unknown to science.

Sharks, skates & rays recipes

< crimped skate >

This English recipe is by Lizzie Heritage and was published in *Cassell's Household Cookery* in 1909. Lizzie Heritage held first-class diplomas in cookery and domestic economy. Here is her recipe in its entirety.

'Skate, Crimped: This is generally sold in slices with a bit of liver in each, tied or fastened in a roll. These may be cooked as they are, or cut into narrower strips, and refastened. They should be put into cold water to cover, with a little vinegar and salt for an hour before boiling, then drained, after boiling as above directed, and served with the same sauce, or brown caper sauce.'

'Another way: This is very delicate eating. Have ready enough fish stock to cover the fish; to a quart, add half a tablespoon each of salt and lemon juice, a sliced carrot and a onion, half a dozen peppercorns, and a sprig of parsley. Boil it up, skim well, lay in the fish, and cook gently. Dish the fish in a pile, and pour over it tomato or parsley sauce, or melted butter, flavoured with lemon juice and herbal vinegar. The fish liquor may be used for soup or souchet.'

Note: Lizzie Heritage gives other ray and skate recipes in this very comprehensive early 20th-century cookbook. She describes skate as being good and wholesome, stating that the young fish are called 'maids' and that they are very delicate. She says that the liver of the fish is valued and when it is boiled it is often added to the sauce.

<stingray panfried with onion, rosemary and chillies, and simmered in apple cider>

SERVES 4

- 1.5 – 2 kg (3 – 4 lbs) fresh stingray or 2 skate wings
- seasoned flour (125 g / 4 oz flour with a tablespoon of paprika, a teaspoon of salt and a teaspoon of white pepper, well mixed and prepared before handling the fish)
- olive oil
- 1 spanish onion (red onion), finely diced
- 2 cloves garlic, finely-chopped
- 1 teaspoon finely-chopped red chilli
- 1 tablespoon chopped fresh rosemary
- 1 litre (35 fl oz) draught apple cider (see note)
- paprika
- 1 teaspoon soft butter
- chilli flowers or curled capsicum (bell pepper) strips and finely-chopped parsley, for serving

This recipe was developed to celebrate the first gastronomic attempt by Europeans with local fare. The rays and boiled leaves of tetragon were eaten on board the *Endeavour,* while it was anchored off Botany Bay, and would have added up to a plain meal. In this recipe, the addition of onions, garlic, chillies and herbs, along with the traditional sailor's ale — cider — add strength and definition of flavour to the fish.

TO PREPARE THE SKATE WINGS

1. Wash the fish well in cold water and leave wet to create a vacuum for the skin to adhere to the work surface (this greatly facilitates filleting).
2. Using a serrated-edged knife, trim the ray flap by slicing off the exposed flesh visible at the thickest part of the wing.
3. Slice off and discard the cartilage at the base of the wing.
4. One wing on the cutting board at a time, turn the flap 'best side' down to fillet the thinner white-skinned underside first. Use a butcher-sharp knife 30 cm (12 in) long for filleting the flesh (with skin) from the cartilage.
6. Turn over to the thicker side and repeat the filleting process.
7. Place the wing fillets flat on the work bench and skin each one by placing the knife between skin and flesh at the outer tip of the wing. Work the knife just 5 cm (2 in) towards the wider end. Hold the skin tight, with the knife in place, and shake the skin vigorously from side to side. The skin will come off effortlessly.

TO COOK THE FISH

1. Dip both sides of each wing fillet into the seasoned flour. Shake off any excess.
2. Heat a generous amount of olive oil in a frying pan.
3. Place the wing fillets into the oil, then heap the onion, garlic, chillies and rosemary on top of the wings. Take care that none of the ingredients falls into the hot oil and burns, especially the garlic. Cook for 3 minutes.
4. Turn the wings over, with topping, and cook for another 3 minutes. Watch for stray morsels of onion or garlic that may start to burn, and remove them.
5. Empty at least half of the cider into the pan. Sprinkle paprika onto the fish and some into the sauce. Cook vigorously for up 10 minutes, until the liquid becomes thick and creamy.
6. Swirl in the butter. Let the fish stand for a minute or two.
7. Serve with chilli flowers, or curled capsicum strips sprinkled with finely-chopped parsley.

Note: Strongbow apple cider is best.

Warwick Kent

Pan-fried stingray with onion, rosemary and chillies, simmered in apple cider.

Tetragon & saltbushes

< Tetragonia tetragonoides, Salicornia australis and Suaeda australi >

Tetragon, samphire and seablite are easy to collect and, during times of economic depression, these green vegetables were eaten from necessity. Largely unused in Australia today, perhaps because they do not lend themselves to mechanical harvesting, they are foods that have nevertheless been readily adopted by European diners. Tetragon may possibly be the original lost opportunity; these leaves could have easily been the first commercial wild food.

tetragon

Jean-Paul Bruneteau

Tetragon (Tetragonia tetragonoides).

Tetragon is a ground creeper with a fleshy stem and glistening bright-green arrowhead-shaped leaves. It is found in coastal regions, on sandy soil around mangroves, and sometimes in the sand dunes of the semi-arid regions of Australia. It is also known as New Zealand spinach or warrigal greens (*warrigal* being an Aboriginal word for 'wild').

Aborigines did not seem to find the plant attractive as a food, possibly because of its high salt content. Like other types of spinach, it is not suitable to be eaten raw because of soluble oxalates but its salinity and oxalate level are reduced when the leaves are boiled. Boiling tetragon also enhances the olive green of the leaves.

Tetragon tastes more like green beans than spinach. This flavour appeals to children who abhor the stronger taste of spinach and silver beet (Swiss chard). It is easily cultivated from seed and becomes self-sowing, earning yet another name: 'perpetual spinach'. It grows well, without need of fertiliser or pesticide, and creates a thick, attractive weed-resistant mat. When grown in the shade of trees, the leaves can attain lengths of 15 to 17 centimetres (six to seven inches). Tetragon can often be found with other edible succulents under casuarina trees fringing tidal waterways.

FORAGING FOR GREENS

In the three years that Lieutenant James Cook, captain of HM Barque *Endeavour*, spent exploring the South Pacific region, none of his crew succumbed to the effect of scurvy. This monumental feat of maritime history was achieved by Cook's pedantic preventative measures: anti-scorbutic food like sauerkraut and malt as well as reduced meat broth (known as portable soup and which resembled stock-cube gum) was issued for all men. In every port of call, officers and crew replenished their supply of wild legumes and other palatable greens under order.

In October 1769 Cook sailed into Queen Charlotte Sound on the windy rugged tip of the South Island of New Zealand, and dropped anchor. A party set off to explore the shore and forage. The leaves of a wild spinach were picked, boiled and eaten. The four-sided seed of this slightly salty plant was recognised as belonging to the *Tetragonia* genus.

Seven months later, at Sting-rays Harbour (later renamed Botany Bay), Joseph Banks (aged 27) and Daniel Solander found the same spinach. The spinach was collected and boiled and found to be the perfect accompaniment to the stingrays served on the eve of the *Endeavour's* departure. Banks remarked of the spinach that it tasted 'as well as spinach or very near it.' The ship was loaded to the brim with over 30 000 samples of fauna and flora collected on this unprecedented epic journey, nearly 1000 of these from Australia. The seeds of the spinach were taken back to England and by 1772 the plant had been successfully propagated in the Royal Botanic Gardens at Kew.

SELF-SUFFICIENT PENAL COLONY

Petty stealing was rampant in London and usually related to survival, food often being the property stolen. Sentences for petty theft were stiff and convict hulks in the Thames were used to house the overflowing convict population. Transportation was considered the best avenue for ridding the nation of this criminal element.

Joseph Banks (now 34) was called to give evidence to a House of Commons Committee in London to determine the possibility of establishing a penal colony in New Holland (Terra Australis). He told the committee that the climate was good, the soil was arable, there was plenty of fresh water and an abundance of fish. 'The grass was long and luxuriant, and there were some eatable Vegetables, particularly a Sort of wild Spinage'.

On Banks's assurance that the colony could be self-sufficient within one year the decision to establish a penal colony at Botany Bay was made.

SUMMER SPINACH

The native spinach was little used in the new colony. In England, however, the leaves of *Tetragonia* were promoted as a 'summer' spinach. In 1821 Mr John Anderson, gardener to the Earl of Essex, read a report to the English Horticultural Society regarding a 'new Esculent Vegetable called Tetragonia'. He said that he had obtained seed stock from Lord Essex, who had got it in Paris, and that he raised the produce through the summer. 'My whole crop in the present year consisted solely of nine plants,' he said, 'and from these I have been enabled to send a gathering for the kitchen every other day since the middle of June, so that I consider a bed with about twenty plant quite sufficient to give a daily supply, if required, for a large table.'

Tetragon seed had been introduced to France by way of the Kew Gardens, and first appeared in American seed catalogues in 1826. Tetragon is now so firmly in place in Europe as a green vegetable that its origin as an introduced plant seems almost forgotten. This plant is now so well established that it is considered a weed in some parts of the world.

saltbushes

Samphire (*Salicornia australis*) and seablite (*Suaeda australis*) have excellent eating qualities. Samphire is used in England for vegetable pickling and, like tetragon, is readily available in the fresh produce markets of provincial France, Italy, Spain and Portugal. In France, the youngest shoots are a popular addition to soup and salads because of their salty flavour and stringless quality.

Seablite is a small shrub with numerous, fragile, up-reaching branches. The tips of seablite and the young shoots of samphire are an excellent salt replacement when fried to a crisp and eaten with fish.

In the journal of John White, Surgeon of the First Fleet, reference is made on 16 August 1788 to native spinach growing on the shoreline along with plants resembling sage, samphire and a small shrub distinguished by the name 'the vegetable tree'. Today those same plants still grow along tidal inland waterways — they are tetragon, seablite, samphire and grey saltbush (*Atriplex cinerea*).

Jean-Paul Bruneteau

Samphire shoots (Salicornia australis).

tetragon & saltbush recipes

<creamed tetragon>

SERVES 6 – 8 AS A SIDE DISH

2 kg (4 lbs) or
1 supermarket carry-bag full of tetragon leaves

butter for frying

1 spanish onion (red onion), finely chopped

2 cloves garlic, minced

salt

ground black pepper

200 ml (6½ fl oz) sour cream

Tetragon can be picked in long tendrils. The tips are kept whole, while larger leaves should be picked off the main stem. Young tetragon plants can be used whole. Creamed tetragon can be served as a vegetable, used as a filling for quiches or as a stuffing.

1. Bring a large pan of unsalted water to the boil, drop in tetragon leaves, bring back to the boil and cook for 2 minutes.
2. Strain, then run the leaves under cold water. Drain and squeeze excess water from a small amount at a time. Chop or mince ready for use.
3. Melt a small amount of butter in a frying pan, then add onion, garlic, pepper and salt. Cook without browning.
4. Add the chopped tetragon. Cook while stirring for 3 minutes.
5. Add sour cream and mix through. Cook for a further 2 minutes.
6. Flatten the mixture into an oven-proof dish and place in the oven for 8 to 10 minutes at 180°C (350°F).

<spiced tetragon pasta>

SERVES 6 – 8

You will need a dough hook and a pasta maker for this recipe.

1. Place the flour into a mixing bowl and make a well in the centre of the flour.
2. Place eggs, salt, cumin and olive oil into the well.
3. Use a dough hook to knead until the dough leaves the sides of the bowl. Continue to beat a further 3 minutes.
4. Remove the dough from the bowl and knead on a floured board.
5. Using a pasta maker, roll out the dough to the third lowest setting. With the pasta ribbon on the floured surface, place tetragon leaves over one half (the right-hand side). Fold the left-hand side of the pasta ribbon over onto the tetragon-covered section, like closing a book. Re-roll, flouring the dough all the time.
6. Keep rolling the sheet to the finest setting on the pasta maker and cut to desired pasta style.
7. Drop the pasta into boiling salted water with some olive oil. Cook until the pasta is *al dente*.

- 400 g (13 oz) plain semolina flour, plus extra for flouring the dough
- 4 x 60 g (2 oz) whole eggs
- 1 teaspoon salt
- 1 tablespoon olive oil, plus extra for cooking the pasta
- ½ teaspoon cumin, finely ground
- 12 large tetragon leaves, blanched and dried

Warwick Kent

Spiced tetragon pasta.

<deep-fried saltbush>

SERVES 6 – 8 AS A GARNISH

- a few handfuls of seablite and/or samphire
- peanut oil for deep frying
- absorbent paper

The stems of samphire develop a central string in midsummer. It is best then to enjoy this plant in early spring when the shoots are young and free of string. Deep-fried saltbush is delicious served on fish, or on any food that can handle a natural salt 'crunch'.

1. Pick the 'leaves' off the saltbushes and deep fry in peanut oil.
2. Drain on absorbent paper.

<tetragon, macadamia and bunya nut pesto>

SERVES 6 – 8

- 5 bunya nuts, boiled, shelled and minced
- 10 whole macadamia nuts, roasted
- 1 handful of blanched, squeezed and chopped tetragon
- 2–3 cloves garlic
- 1 cup roughly chopped basil leaves
- 100 g (3½ oz) grated parmesan cheese
- juice of 2 large lemons
- ½ – ¾ cup (125–180 ml / 4–6 fl oz) olive oil
- salt to taste

Bunya nuts are useful in this recipe to absorb the extra oil thrown out by the macadamia nuts. The bunya nut also softens the pungent flavour of pesto, as well as keeping the pesto firm.

1. In a food processor, blend the bunya and macadamia nuts for 15 seconds.
2. Add tetragon, garlic and basil with the parmesan cheese, add lemon juice and pour in olive oil gradually while blending.
3. Only continue adding oil until the required consistency is achieved — not too runny. Add salt as required.

Warwick Kent

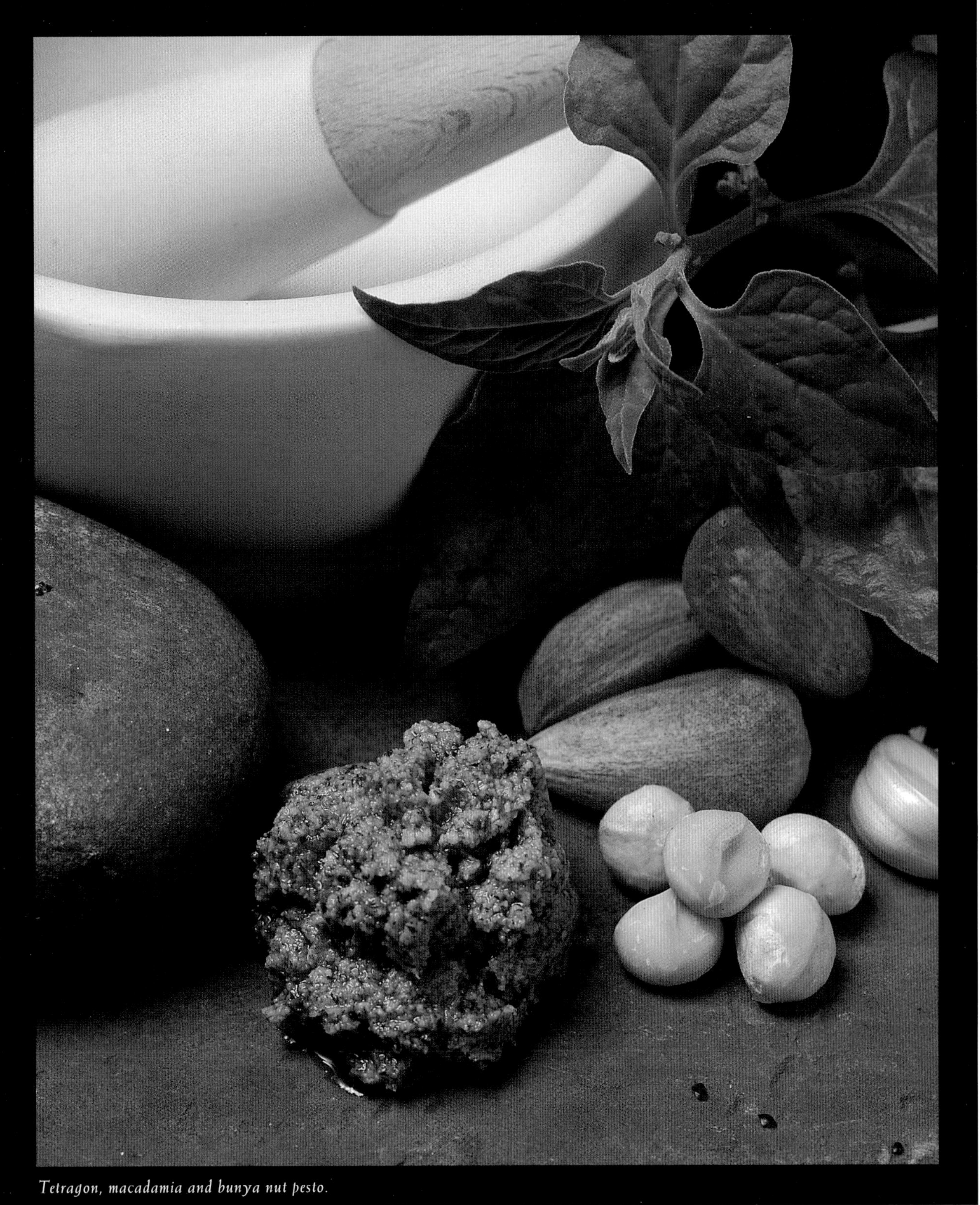

Tetragon, macadamia and bunya nut pesto.

herbs, spices & oils

< Lemon-scented myrtle, native sarsaparilla, sassafras and native mint >

From the dawn of time, the leaves, seeds and flowers of aromatic plants have been used to enhance or mask the taste of certain foods, as well as for tonics and remedies. Perhaps the earliest attempt of formulating a recipe is the infusion of plant material into water.

herb

oil

lemon-scented myrtle

Warwick Kent

Oil of lemon-scented myrtle.

Of all the aromatic leaves, lemon-scented myrtle (*Backhousia citriodora*) is the best to make Australian native herbal tea. Indeed, its lemon-scented leaf is far more interesting and versatile than the Asian lemon grass that has gained so much popularity since the mid–1980s.

During World War Two, because of a shortage of lemon essence, lemon-scented myrtle was used by the Australian soft-drink company Tarax in the manufacture of their lemonade. Unfortunately, high demand for leaves from the wild-tree population led to the demise of this short-lived venture. Lemonade made from lemon-scented myrtle is most flavoursome, and it is sad that this unique Australian flavour is no longer used in soft-drink production.

Lemon-scented myrtle leaves, infused in a teapot like any other tea leaves, make a truly remarkable brew. This refreshing beverage is now very popular and is served in many fine establishments.

When the leaves are dried by hanging in a shaded area they can be used over a long period without any loss of flavour. When the dried leaves are crushed to a powder, their culinary applications become infinite. Powdered lemon-scented myrtle leaf is delightful as a sprinkle on pumpkin soup and it is a perfect accompaniment to seafood. The dried flowerets and seeds also impart a strong lemon scent and taste and can be infused like the leaf. The closely related aniseed myrtle (*Backhousia anisata*) can be powdered and similarly used for its robust aniseed flavour.

The commercial farming of lemon-scented myrtle began in 1991 at

tea leaves, coffee beans

Australia boasts an impressive range of suitable 'ti-trees' — plants from which to make tea — including several species of *Leptospermum*. The flavours vary according to the essential oil of each species. The early settlers, for whom life was unbearable without 'a cuppa', often found the taste of the infusions were too aromatic for their European palates.

Captain James Cook, during his first southern expedition, brewed the leaves of the manuka bush (*Leptospermum scoparium*). It was soon used effectively in the prevention of scurvy.

Ludwig Leichhardt was always keen to try anything, and coffee alternatives were one of his interests. On his famous journey from Moreton Bay to Port Essington 1844–45, he found an excellent coffee substitute: the seeds of the Mackenzie bean (*Canavalia papuana*). Unfortunately, on his second expedition, his botanist Daniel Bunce became violently ill after drinking a brew made from the same plant.

Goomboorian, near Gympie, in Queensland. Dennis and Rosemary Cullen-Archer of Toona Essential Oils have a plantation of 3500 trees that have been grown without the use of pesticides. The plantation provides distilled oil, leaves and seeds for culinary use, as well as for cosmetics and perfumes. The rainforest trees are attracting a large native bird population and provide an environment for at least four varieties of tree-dwelling frogs in an area previously denuded by inappropriate agriculture.

Further down the coast at Murwillumbah a smaller plantation operated by Jeff James of Warrigal Foods of Australia is supplying lemon-scented myrtle solely for the spice market.

There are numerous growers with plantations of up to 250 trees and at least three growers with an excess of 500 trees in the south-east Queensland and northern New South Wales area.

The rediscovered lemon-scented myrtle is appearing on the supermarket shelf as a spice, and also in fancy breads; perhaps in the not-too-distant future it will reappear in lemonade.

Warwick Kent

Selection of oils: (l-r) lemon-scented myrtle, pepperleaf, macadamia, yolla.

native sarsaparilla

To the early settlers, native sarsaparilla (*smilax glyciphilla*) was among the most popular of all the bush teas and was affectionately known as 'sweet tea'. Its flavour resembles liquorice.

Native sarsaparilla was held in high regard by the Surgeon-General, John White, who recorded in 1790 that the tonic was often used for the prevention of scurvy. It is doubtful, however, that the brew was as effective as it was proclaimed to be. For the leaves of this tendrillar vine to be an effective cure for scurvy, a massive quantity of foliage would have been required for a brew.

Native sarsaparilla was one of the earliest colonial medicines and a common article of trade among Sydney herbalists. It remained a popular tea for the best part of the first 100 years of white settlement (it was even exported to China) but, as scurvy disappeared, so did the need for its use.

In the early days of the colony, Aborigines were often seen chewing the pleasantly flavoured leaves. The ripe berries were also desirable — not least because they show traces of a mild narcotic.

Jean-Paul Bruneteau

Sweet sarsaparilla (Smilax glyciphilla).

sassafras

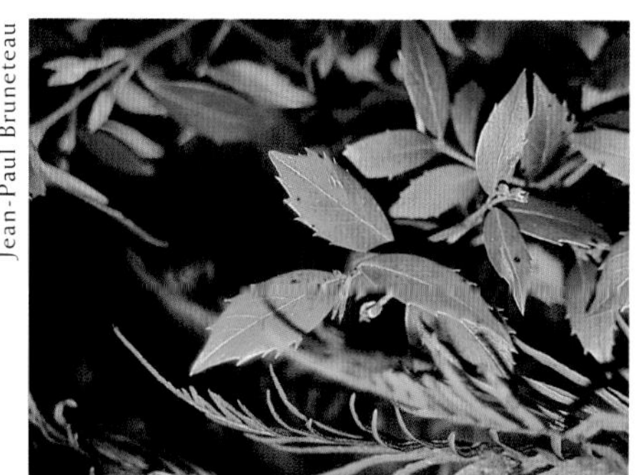
Jean-Paul Bruneteau

Sassafras (atherosperma moschatum).

Sassafras (*atherosperma moschatum*) is another species of considerable culinary interest. These skinny trees grow to 25 m (82 ft) tall and are found at an altitude of about 800 m (2625 ft) in eastern Victoria, eastern New South Wales and in Tasmania, where it is the dominant tree of the western rainforest.

Craftsmen like using sassafras wood for furniture-making, especially for chairs as it is extremely hard and long-lasting.

Sassafras bark is well known for its therapeutic properties and has been used as a tonic and sedative. The bark, which can be used green or dried, makes a decoction which, as it was reported in colonial times, is pleasant when drunk with milk and has a mild laxative effect.

In the mid-1980s, sassafras bark appeared in the bush-food market inappropriately named native nutmeg, no doubt because its aroma was reminiscent of nutmeg. Its flavour, however, has that typical mountain spiciness characteristic of aromatic eucalyptus or menthol, (similar to Tasmanian mountain pepper). Sassafras works well in marinades, and is fantastic rubbed into meats before roasting.

The ale-scented inner bark of the tree can be used to make a homemade brew and is a good yeast substitute in the making of bread.

Paul Jame

Native mint flower (Prostanthea incisa).

native mint

The native mint (*prostanthera incisa*) has delicate leaves and a powerful aroma. Like native sassafras it is compatible with meat.

The leaves of this hardy plant can be used fresh or dried. The dried leaves are suitable for long storage and suffer little loss of potency. Fresh leaves can simply be added to sour cream. Dry leaves can be crushed or powdered and used as a sprinkle, alone or in combination with a number of native herbs and spices.

<sassafras beer>

- 16 litres (28 pints) water
- 4 handfuls of sassafras bark, dried and crushed
- 2 kg (4 lb) granulated sugar
- 150 g (5 oz) brewers yeast
- 100 g (3½ oz) cream of tartar

This is a traditional Tasmanian recipe.

1. Boil water together with the bark for 1 hour.
2. Add sugar, dissolve, then cool the mixture.
3. Add brewers yeast and cream of tartar, stirring with a sterilised spoon.
4. Store for 2 days in a sterilised drum and skim the surface regularly.
5. Strain liquid twice through clean, four-folded muslin.
6. Bottle in sterilised containers, sealing firmly.
7. Store for 6 weeks before sampling.

Note: All equipment in brewing must be sterilised and the brew must be mixed in a clean, non-draughty environment.

<sweet tea>

15 leaves of sarsaparilla
500 ml (16 fl oz) water

1. Leave the sarsaparilla leaves in a dry place for three to four days.
2. When dry, place the leaves in the water, bring to the boil and simmer for 10 minutes.
3. Remove the leaves and pour the infusion into cups; add sugar if desired. Milk is not recommended.

<roast rub>

20% sassafras leaves
20% native mint leaves
50% mountain pepper leaves
10% lemon-scented myrtle leaves

1. Dry each of the leaves by hanging in a warm, ventilated area.
2. Strip the leaves from the stems carefully to avoid bruising.
3. Grind, or hammer mill, each leaf type individually.
4. Blend by sieving the powders together and stir to thoroughly mix.
5. Store in a tightly sealed enamelled tin in the refrigerator.

Note: Over the years, I have tried to duplicate with native herbs the spice blends of the Middle East, India and Asia. Lamb in particular takes easily to herbs and subtle spice treatments which give it an extra dimension. During the initial years of bush-food experimentation each native herb or spice was used on its own for its individual flavour and integrity, but recently I have been melding each to the other, thus creating a new taste sensation.

<lemon-scented myrtle vinegar>

1 litre (35 fl oz) white wine vinegar or rice vinegar
12 dried lemon-scented myrtle leaves

Technically, sour wine vinegar can take up to 24 months to make. It is far more practical to use the manufactured product to create your own flavoured vinegar. For this recipe, you will need sterilised and sealable bottles and a sterilised funnel.

1. Bring vinegar to the boil.
2. Drop leaves into sterilised and sealable bottles.
3. Pour hot vinegar into bottles using a sterilised funnel.
4. Seal bottles while still hot.
5. Leave for a minimum of 1 week before using.

Note: This vinegar is excellent to serve with oysters when it is mixed with finely chopped spanish onion (red onion) and shallots.

Warwick Kent

Ground native spices: (front to back) lemon-scented myrtle, sassafrass, pepperleaf.

<citriodora lollidrops>

150 ml (5 fl oz) water
260 g (8½ oz) granulated sugar
50 ml (2 fl oz) liquid glucose
12 drops of lemon-scented myrtle oil
1 thread of saffron, for colour

For this recipe, you will need a confectionary thermometer and an oiled marble slab. You will also need lollipop sticks (see note).

1. Combine water, sugar and glucose together and bring to the boil.
2. Boil to 148°C (298°F) or soft-crack toffee stage. Test that it has reached this stage by dropping some syrup into iced water. Remove the resulting toffee and gently stretch between fingers. It should separate into hard, pliable and sticky strands.
3. Add the 12 drops of oil and the saffron thread.
4. Remove thread when desired colour is reached.
5. Boil syrup to 152°C (306°F) or hard-crack stage. Hard crack is tested by dropping syrup into iced water. This time the toffee should snap and not feel sticky.
6. Pour a spoonful at a time of syrup onto an oiled marble slab. Press a lollipop stick into each drop. If desired, a cut leaf-tip of lemon-scented myrtle can be pressed in with the stick. An additional drop over the stick will secure the lollidrop.
7. Remove the lollidrops from the marble by using a sharp, shovel-nosed scraper.
8. Lollidrops should be wrapped in cellophane and kept in an air-tight container.

Note: Lollipop sticks can be difficult to purchase but they are simple and inexpensive to make. Cut wooden satay skewers to the appropriate length and cover these with rice paper or with a strip of paper (about 1 cm / ½ in wide) cut from a white paper bag. Dampen the paper strips and firmly twist a strip around each of the skewers by turning the skewers between your fingers. When dried, the rolled paper should hold firmly and the sticks can be used.

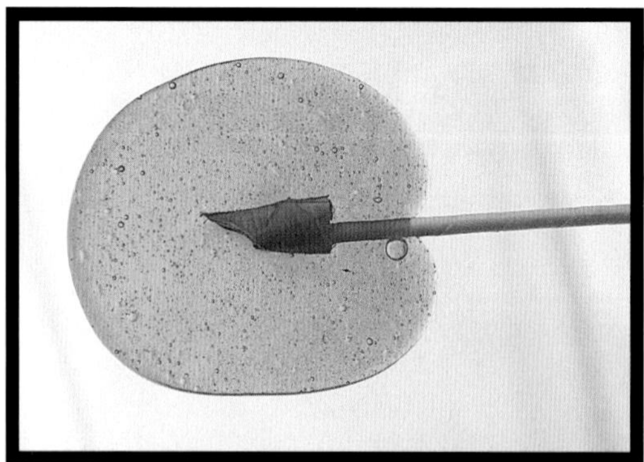

Warwick Kent

Citriodora lollipops.

Macadamia

< *Macadamia integrifolia* and *Macadamia tetraphylla* >

There are several species of macadamia worldwide, of which five are endemic to Australia. The preferred commercial species are *Macadamia tetraphylla* **(native to northern New South Wales) and** *Macadamia integrifolia* **(native to Queensland). Macadamias were the first Australian native trees to be developed as a food crop. In 1882** *Macadamia integrifolia* **found its way to Hawaii, where its botanical name** *Macadamia* **was used as a trade name to market Australia's native nut. Several varieties of the tree were developed on the island of Oahu, and these have come to Australia with their Hawaiian names: Ikaika, Kakea, Keaau and Keauhou.**

hard nut, brittle tree

An Aboriginal name for the macadamia nut is *kindal kindal*; it is also known as bauple nut, bopple nut and Queensland nut. It is the world's hardest nut to crack and is considered the best eating.

Macadamias occur naturally in the area between Gympie and Maryborough in Queensland, to the north of bunya bunya country, centring on Mount Bauple. In 1995 the Mount Bauple area boasted at least three commercial nut enterprises.

Macadamia integrifolia has a higher oil content and is the most popular commercial variety. Its nut has a smooth shell. *Macadamia tetraphylla* is also grown commercially for the fresh nut trade. Its nut is sweeter, and has a pebble appearance and a rough shell. This tree is more suited to the home garden as it withstands lower temperatures and is more robust.

Macadamias are very attractive though brittle trees. A mature tree attains a height of 20 m (66 ft). Its leaves are dark green, elongated, toothed and usually occur in whorls of three or four. Flowers appear in spring: *Macadamia integrifolia* has white flowers and *Macadamia tetraphylla* has pink flowers. The flowers are on racemes about 25 cm (10 in) long, each raceme having as many as 10 nuts which develop to maturity from early autumn to mid-winter (March to July).

The green leathery husks usually split when the nuts are mature, revealing a glimpse of the hard brown nut inside. Nuts are at their best when left to fall from the tree, as this ensures that their oil content is at its highest. At this stage, removal of the remaining husk is relatively easy. An immature nut-in-shell will float, while a mature nut-in-shell sinks.

forecast

The plantation area of commerically developed macadamia trees in Australia now exceeds 20 000 hectares, with over three million trees from the mid-north coast of New South Wales to the Atherton Tablelands of Northern Queensland, plus a few minor plantings in Western Australia. By 1995 Australia was exporting its product to nearly 40 countries and had developed a reputation for quality and reliability. In that year, it was estimated that by the year 2000, Australia would be the largest producer and supplier of premium-grade macadamia nuts to the world.

against the odds

To the north of Sydney, along Wyong Creek at Yarramalong, a 900-tree plantation of mixed *Macadamia* varieties has been developed. In spite of the odds against success, Barkala was begun in the 1970s as the southern-most commercial plantation in Australia. Wind and frost killed some trees in the early days, but losses were minimal. The rainforest trees have grown well and today Barkala Plantation's product is second to none.

The owners George and Elizabeth Rakusan prefer to use organic methods to produce their fine crop.

The mature nuts are allowed to fall from the trees to maximise their oil content. After the remains of the leathery husks are removed, the nuts are dried in drying towers for two weeks. Large fans force air through the nuts, reducing the moisture content by half. The nuts are then transferred to hot-air driers for five days, reducing the moisture further. The nuts are ready when the kernels rattle in the shell. George was pioneering this method of drying and constructing his own purpose-built equipment, while the rest of the industry was still using rack-drying methods.

the good nut

Macadamia nuts can be eaten raw, salted, dry roasted, or roasted with coconut or macadamia oil. They contain absolutely no cholesterol, possess anti-oxidant properties and are high in calcium and vitamin B. Nutritionists suggest that a

Warwick Kent

crackers

Bart's Original Nut Kracker (better known as the BONK) is a clever yet simple device for cracking the macadamia's hard shell without damaging the nut. This hand-held vice allows variable pressure to be applied while securely holding the nut, which could otherwise become a dangerous missile.

With practice, a whole nut may be retrieved using the Automatic Macadamia Opener crafted by George Rakusan. This tool is lathed from a solid brass rod weighing close to one kilogram (two pounds), which is then made into two pieces. A hollow in one piece holds the nut while the hand-held striker shatters the shell on impact.

Warwick Kent

Gundabluey Bushfood Macadamia Nut Oil.

daily dietary supplement of six to 20 macadamias can help reduce heart disease, lowering blood triglycerides and blood cholesterol by seven per cent in four weeks. The energy count is 2960 kilojoules (707 calories) for each 100 g (3½ oz) of nuts.

Around 75 per cent of the nut's weight can be recovered as high-quality, cold-pressed oil. Macadamia oil is higher in mono-unsaturated fats than olive oil and is flavoursome and distinctive, but can easily dominate other flavours.

john macadam

Born in May 1827 at Northbank near Glasgow, Scotland, John Macadam arrived in Australia on the *Admiral* in 1855 to take up a teaching post in chemistry at Scotch College, Melbourne. In 1858 he was appointed to the office of Government Analytical Chemist and entrusted with medico-legal investigations. Two years later he became Health Officer, engaged in analysis of food and drink.

Throughout his life Macadam was in constant poor health. His workload and commitment to his many offices contributed to his death at the age of 38 on board the *Alhambra* while on his way to New Zealand to testify for the second time in a murder trial. Macadam's untimely death on 2 September, 1865 occurred a mere 10 years after his arrival in the colony. On 5 August 1857, the famous botanist Dr von Mueller honoured Macadam by giving the name macadamia to the newly recognised genus of the family *Proteaceae*.

<dry roasted nuts>

1 kg (2 lb) macadamia nuts in shell

This method of dry roasting macadamia nuts has been developed by Elizabeth Rakusan of the Yarramalong Macadamia Nut Farm. Dry roasting your own macadamias will ensure the cholesterol-lowering properties are not diminished. Commercially-available nuts are often roasted in macadamia or coconut oil. Elizabeth's method for dry roasting nuts produces a tastier and crisper result, allowing the full, unadulterated flavour of the nut to come through. Purchased nuts in shells have been air dried to reduce their moisture content by half and allow the kernel to come cleanly away from the shell. Bart's Original Nut Kracker (BONK) is a practical tool which opens the macadamia's nuts without damaging the kernels.

1. Place shelled nuts on clean, dry, scone trays in a fan-forced oven at 120°C (250°F). After one hour turn and roast them for another hour.
2. Allow to cool. Store in an air-tight container.

<elizabeth's chocolate coated macadamia nuts>

This is Elizabeth's recipe for her famous (and delicious) home-dipped, chocolate-coated macadamia nuts.

'After the nuts are dry roasted, we select the largest nuts for dipping in chocolate. We melt a good-quality compound chocolate over a double boiler, being careful not to let it get too hot, else it will thicken. The burner is turned to low and when hot enough turned off. Add a cup of nuts and stir with a knife. The coated nuts are picked out with tweezers and put in rows on stainless-steel trays to set.

Nuts for ever, Elizabeth R.'

<macadamia nut tuiles>

100 g (3½ oz) caster sugar (superfine granulated sugar)

2 egg whites

3 drops vanilla essence

50 g (2 oz) plain flour (all-purpose flour)

50 g (2 oz) butter, softened

1 tablespoon macadamia nuts, lightly roasted and crumbed

50 g (2 oz) chocolate, melted

A tuile is named for its shape, *tuile* being French for terracotta roof tile. The light biscuits are crisp, sugary and brittle. They are shaped over a rolling pin while hot and left to harden.

1. Beat the sugar and egg whites for 3 to 4 minutes.
2. Add the vanilla essence.
3. Fold in the flour.
4. Add the softened butter.
5. Add crumbed nuts and fold through.
6. Spoon the mixture onto a heavy greased tray, 1 or 2 spoonfuls at a time, and then spread thinly.
7. Drizzle with melted chocolate.
8. Cook at 190°C (375°F) for about 3 to 4 minutes until the mixture is cooked in the centre and golden at the edges.
9. While the biscuits are still hot, lift them off the tray with the aid of the wide-edged paint scraper, and place them immediately over a rolling pin. Allow the shaped biscuits to harden before removing.

Warwick Kent

Macadamia nut tuiles.

<macadamia nut praline>

1 cup (220 g / 7 oz) caster sugar (superfine granulated sugar)

1 cup (250 ml / 8 fl oz) water

1 cup or 220 g (7oz) macadamia nut chips, medium roasted

Praline, once known as *prasline*, originated in France. Lassagne, a member of the household of the Duc de Choiseul-Praslin, was responsible for refining the process that started with children caramelising almonds stolen from the kitchen of the Duc. Lassagne protected the children in return for some of the treats. These so impressed him that he perfected the confection and presented it to the King of France, passing it off as his own. Lassagne went on to open a confectionery shop in Montargis, named *Maison de la Prasline*, which still exists today.

1. In a sugar pan or heavy-based saucepan, place the sugar and water together and cook, without stirring, on medium heat until all the sugar is dissolved.
2. When the sugar syrup is clear, place a warmed sugar thermometer in the pan and boil evenly at medium to high without stirring.
3. Cook until the mixture is honey coloured, at 165°C (330°F), or light caramel stage.
4. Arrange nuts, fairly close together, on a lightly oiled marble slab, a greased, heavy stainless-steel tray, or a sugar mat.
5. Pour toffee over the nuts and leave to set.
6. When cool, break into small chunks, which in turn may be chopped finely for sprinkling.

Warwick Kent

Macadamia nut praline, broken on a plate.

Cider gum, sugarbag & hard yacca

It is not only the fruits, leaves and bark of trees that offer edible delights from the bush. The 'juice' — the sap exuded from some Australian trees — also has its own delicious and practical uses.

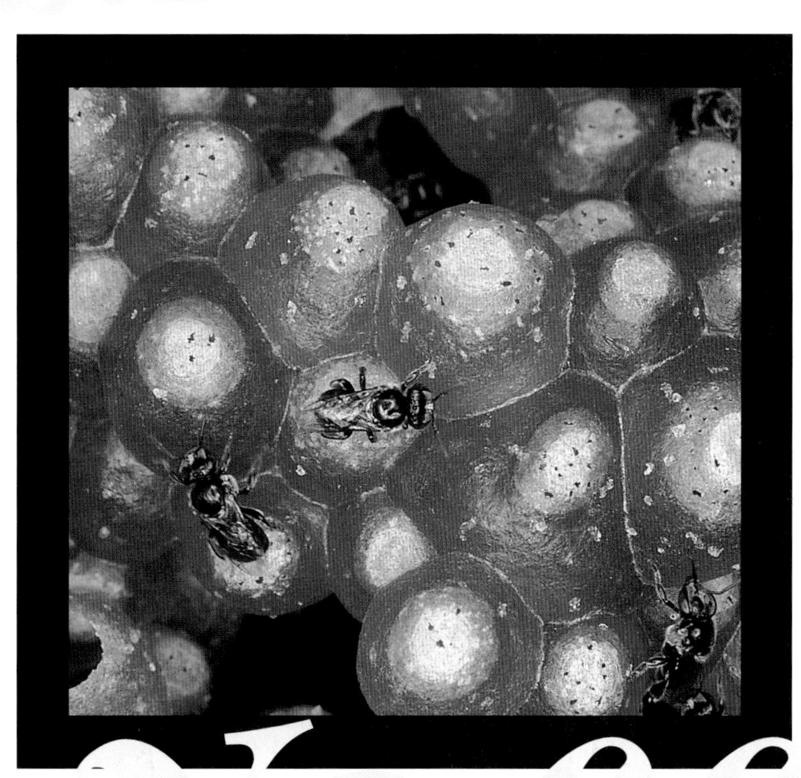

Warwick Kent

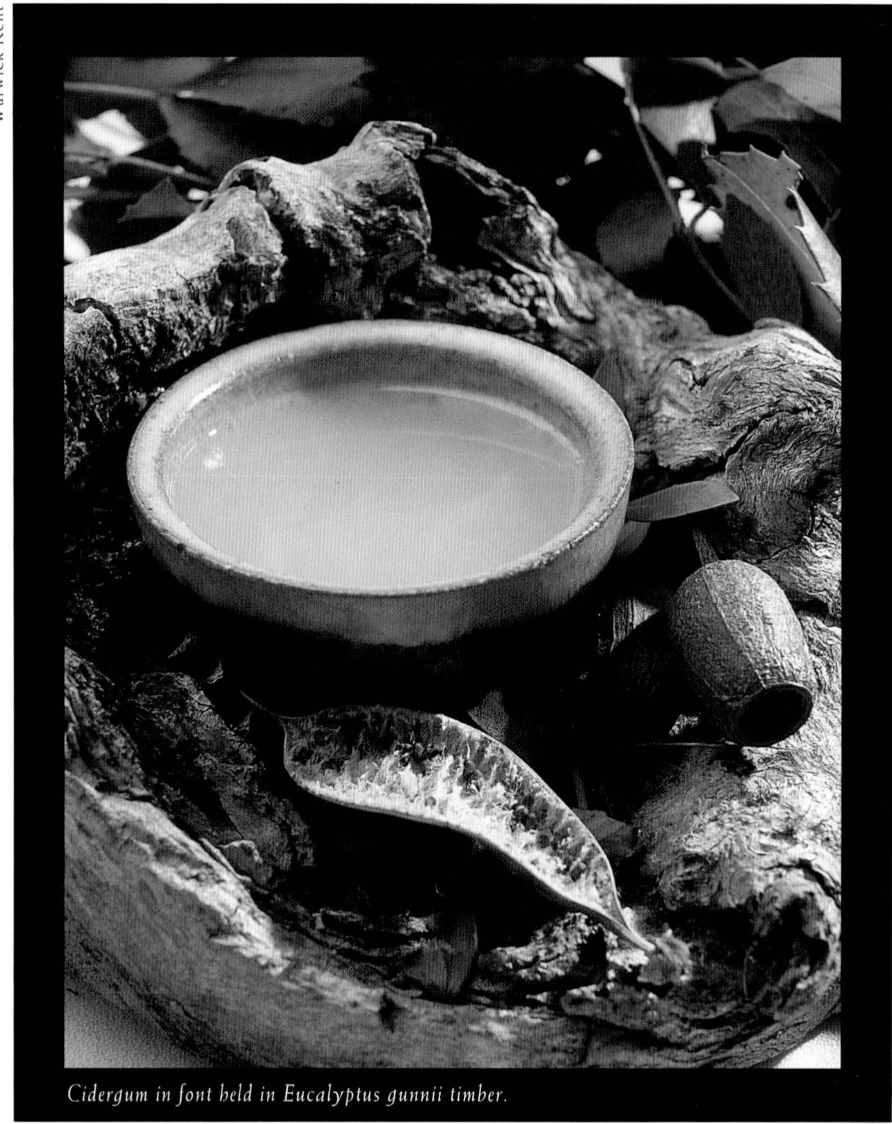

Cidergum in font held in Eucalyptus gunnii timber.

cider gum (eucalyptus gunnii)

In late summer, the cider gum begins to exude an extraordinary and sweet substance equal in taste to the best Canadian maple syrup. This tree is found only in Tasmania, where it occurs on the margins of treeless areas on dolerite mountains.

EXTRAORDINARY SAP

The Aborigines living on Tasmania's Cradle Mountain called this sweet sap *wayalinah*, and carved out receptacles at the base of some trees to collect the honey-coloured nectar. These scars are still visible today on the trunks of very old trees. The sap was collected in a dug-out trough lined with clay and covered with a piece of bark or a flat stone to protect the liquid from birds and other animals.

MOUNTAIN CIDER

The cider gum visually resembles some other eucalypts but the smell makes its identification unmistakable. The stale odour of cider is very noticeable at close range when the syrup oozes from fissures and scars, some of these probably created by birds and animals eager to share in the feast. Growing among large scattered rocks in fertile soil, at an altitude of between 600 and 1100 m (2000 and 3600 ft), the trees are subject to heavy snowfalls. With no less than 150 frosts a year, the temperature never reaches more than 20° C (68° F) and it is believed that the sweet free-flowing sap is the tree's anti-freeze.

I have had the privilege of being shown magnificent old specimens on the central plateau of Tasmania by Stephen Harris, the botanist credited with drawing the attention of the bush food industry to *E. gunnii*. Stephen Harris has quoted one observer as saying the flavour is 'just like Cointreau, very sweet with a faint fruity orange essence and flavour'. I think it tastes more like maple syrup. Ironically, University of Tasmania research is being used in France to cultivate *E. gunnii* in high altitude plantations for timber only without showing any interest so far in the sap. This sensational natural elixir is by far one of the sweetest encounters I have experienced among Australian wild foods.

The fermented brew of *E. gunnii* sap appears opaque and cloudy in contrast to the clear, freshly-collected, colourless

Nature Focus Library / Thomas Dick Collection

Aboriginal man removing a knobby protuberance from the tree trunk. These were often used as water and honey carriers.

sap. The fermentation of cider gum in a glass bottle generates a lot of gas, which carbonates the drink. If the bottle is open while warm, most of the contents will escape as quickly as champagne would if it were shaken. Until the air-

intoxicating

When cider gum syrup is left to settle it ferments quickly, creating an intoxicating liquor that smells and tastes like apple cider — hence the name cider gum. Aborigines and early settlers knew the properties of the fermented sap only too well. In 1857, the botanist Daniel Bunce stated, 'when allowed to remain any length of time, it ferments and settles into a coarse kind of wine or cider, rather intoxicating if drunk in excess'.

borne yeasts that destabilise the sap so quickly are identified and controlled, this excessive fermentation process presents a major drawback to the development of a cider gum industry. After a year of refrigeration my collected cider continued to ferment.

In Tasmania, no commercial ventures based around the production of cider gum exist. At Tarnuk Bushfoods and Flowers in Gippsland, Victoria, Gil and Meredith Freeman with their son Rhys, a nurseryman, planted 1500 *E. gunnii* in 1988. With the intention of being able to produce the first batch of syrup by the year 2000, Gil estimates the trees will need to be 10 to 15 centimetres (four to six inches) in diameter before the trunks are tapped for their syrup. The seed stock for the cider gum forest was collected in Tasmania from 116 trees in 35 different locations. The seed was collected in this manner to diversify the gene pool. The trees are planted in a block formation with the mountain pepper, *Tasmannia lanceolata*, and *Acacia retnodes*, a wattle with a seed that is very good eating.

Further west, near Lake Eildon, Arthur Marsh planted close to 3000 trees in 1992. Arthur shares information with the Freemans regarding the eventual tapping of the gums, his ideas largely based on his first-hand experience with maple plantations in Canada. The success of these large-scale projects depends on further research to control the air-borne yeasts that trigger the rapid fermentation of the golden secretion. Tasmanian cider gum will become one of the world's favourite natural syrups, especially as production of maple syrup in the northern hemisphere is suffering the effects of continuous acid rain.

Jennifer Isaacs

Wild honey collected in a paperbark coolamon

sugarbag honey

Among the sweet nectars of the Australian bush, the honey produced by the tiny native stingless bee is highly prized. Various Aboriginal communities know the bee as *cooba*, *kuyan* and *warra-nunna* and its honey as *wirotheree*, *quangulnarang* and *willoring*. Today it is better known as sugarbag, a word derived from the colonial hessian sugar bag. The sweetness of honey was related to the taste of sugar, and the word sugarbag substituted by whites for native honey. Honey is an important traditional food for Aborigines, always eaten raw and never cooked or mixed with another food. Honey is collected by a variety of ingenious methods which vary with people and location. Paperbark carriers and wooden bowls made from knobby protuberances of gum trees are useful to carry and store the dark fluid, which usually contains a mixture of pollen balls, wax, tree material and dead bees.

NATURE'S LITTLE HELPERS

The native bees resemble slow-moving, small flies and appear to drift along rather than purposefully bustle about like the introduced bee.

The bees are so small that it takes a trained eye to track down the insignificant entrance to their hive, which features a small 'drop zone' for their clumsy landings. These effective little pollinaters of many of Australia's small flowers will harmlessly crash land onto intruders near their hive. Not confined to making their home in trees, native bees also nest in hollow logs and rock crevices. The very dark honeycomb consists of irregularly-shaped cells within a rough mass of wax. The wax — a tradable commodity in the Kimberleys — is used as a sealant for paperbark carriers.

The flavour and colour of sugarbag will vary according to the plant material available within a region; however, the native honey has a citrus overtone and is less viscous than that produced by introduced bees. Often these hives will be found around macadamia stands, as the bees seem particularly fond of the nectar from the small flowers. The tiny size of the native bee allows it closer contact with the stigma of the flower, ensuring the best chance of fertilisation. Their effective pollination of the macadamia has led to the development of small apiaries to house *Trigonia carbonaria*. Although the bee is adaptable to an artificial hive environment, little has been done, regrettably, to produce sugarbag honey in useful quantities. An apiary of stingless bees can easily be placed within a native garden, giving the observant gardener pleasure while his or her plants are more effectively pollinated, as well as the added bonus of a great honey.

hard yacca

Uses of edible gums from acacias and eucalypts are well-recorded in indigenous and early colonial life, and are often referred to as 'chewing gums'. Some are believed to have medicinal qualities. The yacca gum is of particular interest, although it does not have many culinary applications. The use of yacca gum, its hardness and the effort it takes to collect has caused the term 'hard yakka' to be added the Australian colloquial language. Yacca gum is the resin obtained from 'grass trees' of the *Xanthorrhoea spp*. The grass trees are easily recognised by their tall, straight, single spear flower, the shaft of which is often employed as a spear.

The grass tree does have edible parts: the small white flowers offer a sweet nectar and the centre of the crown has been described as fresh and palatable. The pith of the tree produces a saccharine juice that can be distilled into a proof spirit. However, the resin is by far the main product of the plant, it being one quarter by weight of gum.

While the indigenous people collected the gum from the base of the grass tree, colonial collection methods were much more devastating, destroying the entire plant in the process. Even the tough yellow wood (which turns well) was used to make wasteful souvenir items. Fortunately, the beauty of these majestic long-living trees is recognised today and they are left where they stand to be admired and allowed to produce the hard yacca for which they are famous.

Cider gum, sugarbag & hard yacca recipe

<macadamia nut waffles with sugarbag honey>

½ cup of macadamia nut chips

1 sachet dry yeast

2 cups (500 ml / 16 fl oz) lukewarm milk

2½ cups (310 g / 10 oz) plain flour (all-purpose flour)

1 tablespoon caster sugar (superfine granulated sugar)

2 pinches salt

3 tablespoons melted butter

¼ cup (60 ml / 2 fl oz) macadamia nut oil

4 egg whites

extra macadamia nut oil

6 drops vanilla essence

sugarbag honey to taste

icing sugar (confectioners' sugar) for dusting

Waffles are ancient. They are referred to in poetry of the late 12th century, during which time waffle irons were cast to represent a number of religious observances. The recipe for these light pastries originates in Belgium.

1. Roast the nut chips in a frying pan or in the oven until they are golden brown. Chop finely until they resemble breadcrumbs.
2. Dissolve the yeast in warm milk.
3. Add the sifted flour, sugar, salt and nuts; whisk in well.
5. Pour the cool, melted butter and oil into the mixture. Add vanilla essence.
6. Stir in a quarter of the stiffly-beaten egg whites.
7. Fold in the remainder of the stiff whites.
8. Allow to stand for 45 minutes.
9. Grease a hot waffle iron with oil and pour on enough mixture to adequately cover one surface. Cook each side for approximately 3 minutes. Remove the waffle from the iron, drizzle sugarbag honey over the top and dust with icing sugar.

Warwick Kent

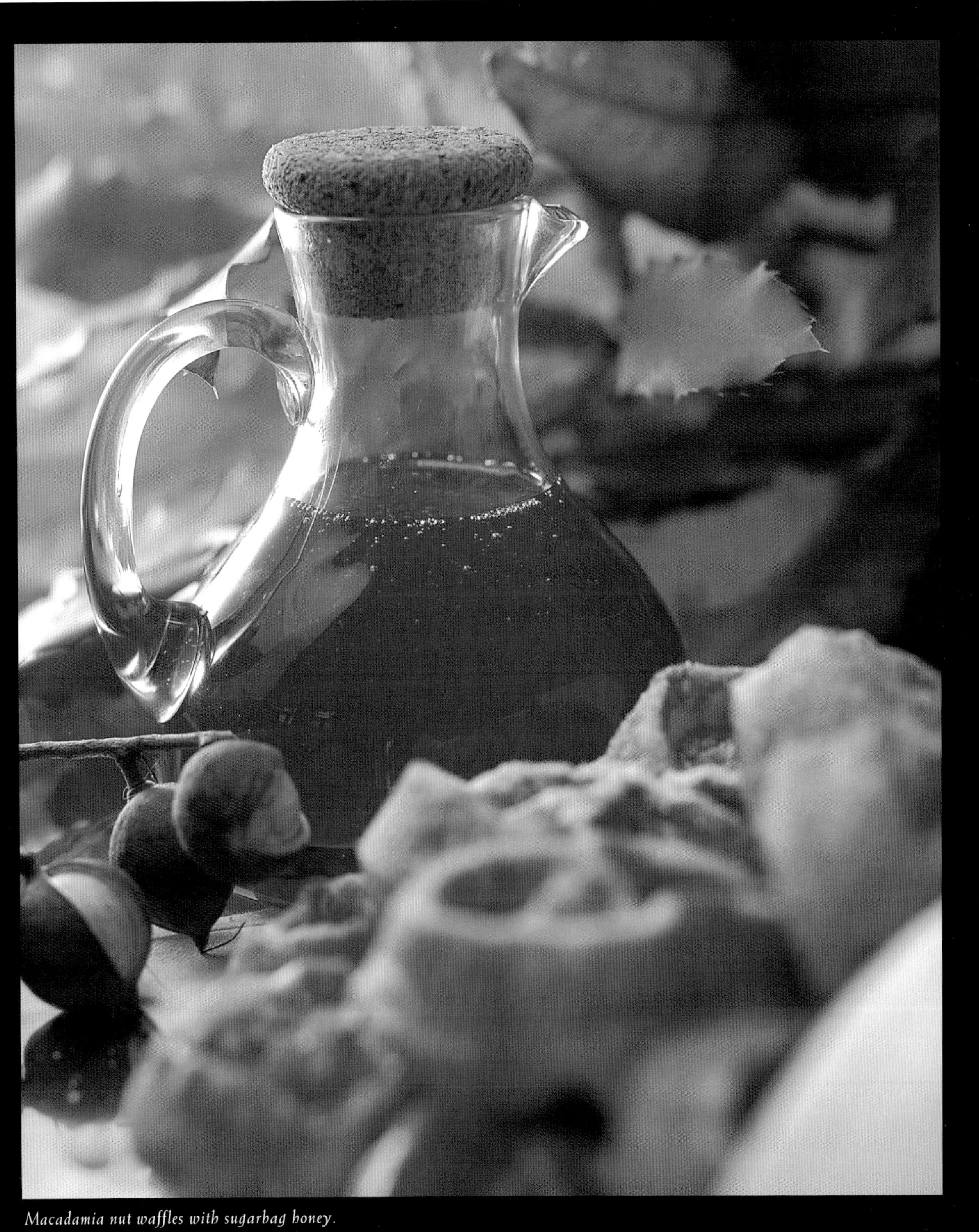

Macadamia nut waffles with sugarbag honey.

Sweet berries & sour fruits

First settlers arrived across the waters from south-east Asia around 60 000 years ago with little food, no domesticated animals and no food plants for cultivation. They encountered food forests of many unfamiliar but usable plant foods which helped to sustain them, supplementing the animal foods they hunted. The fruits and berries of some plants would have been readily adopted as food sources while others were rejected due to their unpleasant taste or poisonous nature, or else they were used more for their therapeutic qualities. The abundant nature and high nutritional value of the wild-food corridors sustained these people in their nomadic lifestyle. The food gathering and land-management practices of the early inhabitants ensured the continued existence of the unique flora.

The settlers arrived in very basic water craft, possibly made from bamboo. They probably expected to find bamboo in Australia which would have allowed them to build new craft for a return journey, but in actual fact may effectively have marooned themselves. It is generally acknowledged that settlement throughout Australia, to the southern tip of Tasmania, took around 20 000 years to complete.

lillipillies

Acmena and *Syzygium spp*, are some of the most abundant fruit-bearing trees found in Australia with some 60 species, the majority of which have edible fruit. Trees of this family would have been encountered very early on by the new arrivals, with further species continuing to be discovered as these people roamed throughout the continent. The fruit vary in taste from bland to fragrant and their texture is crisp and watery like watermelon. Prominent among *Syzygium spp* are clove-scented lillipillies, or riberries, a renowned fruit known for its resilience to overcooking.

This versatile *Syzygium* ('syzygy' meaning the meeting of two heavenly bodies) has been known by a host of other names. The cherry alder, the small-leaved water gum and the clove lillipilli are just some of the names of the riberry, which is a common ornamental tree in large suburban gardens of Queensland and New South Wales.

As an edible fruit tree species, the riberry is regaining its popularity. In 1987 Peter Hardwick, from the New South Wales north coast, introduced riberries as a native rainforest fruit in punnets of 200 grams (6 ½ ounces) accompanied by four recipes. The environmentally conscious Hardwick recommended the packaging from his wild-food product be used as a seed planting tray. From this initial marketing experiment, the riberry has gained a formidable reputation as a bush food, with widespread acceptance.

chameleon

The riberry is most interesting to work with. When the fruits are collected and frozen they turn from their scarlet-red to purple-mauve. If the fruit is accidentally left to thaw, the colour will wash out to a pale lifeless pink and the fruit shrivels. Cooked from frozen, with a little lemon or lime juice in water, the fruit will lose all colour, becoming almost white, miraculously regaining on cooling its rosy-red hue. The fruit can appear a little shrivelled but if it is left in its liquor overnight it will plump out. If sugar is gradually and repeatedly added to the strained liquor, reheated and poured back, the fruit will firm and become translucent with intensifying colour. Repeating this process daily for approximately a fortnight will give an optimum glacé result. When the fruits are drained, the red syrup makes a fantastic base for confectionery. The clove, cousin to the riberry, is an excellent flavour accentuator and the addition of a tiny amount to the cooked fruit is beneficial.

resilient riberry

An accidental discovery demonstrated that this quaint little fruit can endure a great deal of cooking. Once my entire seasonal batch of riberries was left cooking for the best part of 45 minutes, while yours truly was detained by the telephone. The liquor had almost evaporated but, amazingly, the fruit had not collapsed. After cooling overnight, the fruit regained its vigour and retained its full flavour. The riberry is an exceptional, flavoursome fruit and epitomises the versatility of Australian wild foods.

lemon aspen

Another rainforest fruit is the lemon aspen, *Acronychia acidula*. These fruit are about 20 mm (¾ in) in diameter, grapefruit yellow, with a corrugated surface, and grow on canopy trees that may reach anywhere between 5 and 30 m (16 and 98 ft) in height, depending on conditions. Endemic to pockets of the Atherton and Evelyn Tablelands region of Far North Queensland, most fruit is collected from the smaller fringe trees which receive greatest light within the rainforest.

The fruit is ready to harvest from April to September, depending on the climatic conditions which have a major effect on the quantity and quality of the fruit. Ample rainfall is essential for an abundant crop of good-sized fruit with a palatable flavour and lower acidity. Collection of the fruit is labour intensive and pole pickers are utilised in harvesting the fruit from trees that are too dangerous to climb because of mosses and lichens coating the trunk and branches. Unfortunately, the lemon aspen is extremely prone to grub infestation. Mark Peverill, a wild-food harvester, reports that from his 1994 crop of 6000 kilos, two-thirds was unusable. The waste fruit was returned to the rainforest as compost.

The crushed leaves of *Acronychia acidula* smell of turpentine mangoes. This is mirrored in the juice of the fruit which is a potent, almost nauseating grapefruit essence. For this reason, lemon aspens are best processed using the same glacé technique as used for the riberry. My observation of lemon aspen is that a little cooking, plus repeated sugar saturation, softens the strong flavour of the lemon aspen. Unlike the riberry, which is pleasant and refreshing in its raw state, the lemon aspen is better suited to cooking. The tiny, crunchy, black seeds of the aspen are encased in a plastic-like covering. The seeds themselves are edible and attractive, but the covering needs discarding as it is unpleasant and irritating to chew. The syrup left over from glacéing is ideal as a cordial. The flavour of lemon aspen is excellent in fruit curds and salad dressings.

davidson plum

Known as the 'Queen of the Rainforest' is the large, deep-purple Davidson Plum, *Davidsonia pruriens*. This very sour plum makes the best bush-fruit jam or jelly, and an excellent plum wine. The juice is indeed so sour that perhaps its greatest use is as an alternative to the vinegar required in tangy salad dressings. Two variations of plums are found within the same species, the smooth Davidsonia and the more common hairy variety. The latter has fine golden irritant hairs which are easily removed by gently rubbing under running water. The fruit contains two flat seeds, only one of which appears firm and fertile. Unfortunately, the flesh clings strongly to the these. The tree on which this fruit can be found is a treat to the eye when it shoots its new crown of velvety crimson-red leaves. The new growth contrasts with the older dark green toothed pinnate leaves, which lose their felt-like underside covering with time.

tamarinds

Tim Low

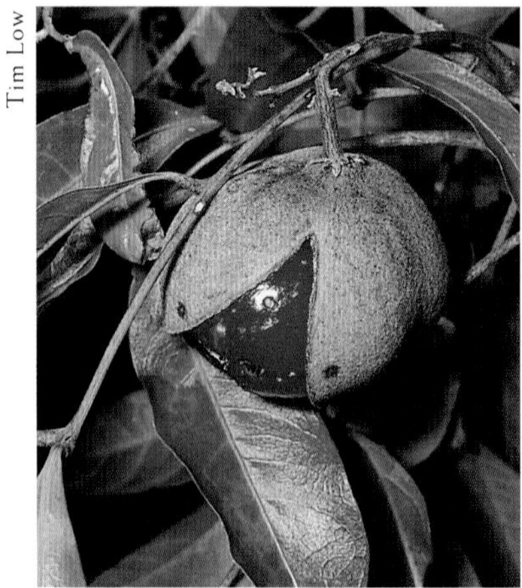

Native tamarind (Diploglottis campbellii).

There are two other sour fruits worth a mention, although they are difficult to process because their minimal soft flesh clings to a very large stone. The native tamarinds, *Diploglottis campbellii* and *D. australis*, of tropical and sub-tropical regions are exquisite. Their zinging acidic flavour works well with the cooked flesh of large flaked fish such as barramundi and, when combined with butter as a *beurre composé* is excellent on steaks.

rosellas

In the same region there is a popular 'adopted wild food', the rosella, *Hibiscus sabdariffa*. The rosella is a flowerbud of an annual that grows to two metres (6 feet) in tropical and sub-tropical climates. This cultivated plant is closely related to our own native yellow or white hibiscus, *H. heterophyllus*. The flower of the native plant is bland in comparison to the bright red North African introduced species. The fleshy petals of rosella surround a large green inedible seed pod that needs to be removed by cutting at the base of the flower. The remaining petals hold well and can be frozen for later use without any loss of colour or flavour. The raw flavour is tart and slightly sour. With added sugar, the petals can convert to a wonderful jelly without requiring pectin. Jam and chutneys made from the petals are equally flavoursome. Glacé rosella petals are crisp and colourful crown garnishes for desserts, and are easily made using the same glacé process as for riberries and lemon aspens.

Once very popular, many recipes using rosellas have been published over the years. In summer whole rosellas can be found at the fresh fruit and vegetable markets of Australian capital cities. Although not a cheap commodity the rosella is well worth rediscovering.

muntries

Away from the rainforest and into coastal South Australia and the coastal region of western Victoria, the remarkable muntrie, *Kunzea pomifera*, is found. This exposed plant carpets the dunes with its woody trailing creepers. The white flowers of spring are followed by small burgundy-red and green fruit smothered by a fine non-irritating fluff. The summer air is heavy with the ripe aroma of apples as if in an orchard. Their refreshing good taste and easy picking made muntries popular with both Aborigines and white settlers. In late summer, tribes would converge on the coast, coming from as far as inland Victoria to feast on the monterry, munter or *ngurp* as they were known, taking whole creepers away with them. The settlers to the area also relished muntries in jams and tarts.

The wild fruit may be collected from the South Australian dunes with a permit obtainable from the Department of Environment and Natural Resources in that state. It is hoped that the use of such permits will encourage gatherers to be responsible in the quantities of fruit they take and the methods they use to collect. They are also encouraged to show respect for the fragile environment of this dune-stabilising plant.

Muntries have excellent prospects of becoming a commercially viable fresh fruit crop and are currently receiving special attention from Diane and Roger Fielke who have established Australia's first bushfood nursery to supply native plant material to growers.

James Vandepeer, a wheat, barley, sheep and cattle farmer on the Yorke Peninsular at Ardrossan, South Australia, has planted 1700 of the Fielke's propagated stock in the first commercial *Kunzea pomifera* enterprise. Although the plant is not endemic to the Yorke Peninsula it appears particularly suited to this area because of the coastal climatic conditions of the Vandepeer land which receives onshore winds from Spencer Gulf and the Gulf of St Vincent. Pest problems have not yet been encountered at this early stage and the watering requirements have been minimal. First harvest of muntries was in early 1996, when small amounts were collected. When peak production is achieved the crop will produce around two tonnes, each plant bearing one to one and a half kilograms.

Tim Low

Muntries (Kunzea pomifera), Beachport, South Australia.

Freezing, in my opinion, does not suit this fruit. Like frozen apples, the thawed product is mushy and brown. Dry freezing, however, does give a crisp and tasty result, but the process is not presently economically viable.

The name, *Kunzea pomifera,* implies a similarity to the apple or *pomme.* Unfortunately, muntries are being likened to cranberries which could not be further from the truth. Brother of Roger Fielke, chef Andrew Fielke of the

Paul James

Snowberries (Gaultheria hispida).

Red Ochre Grill Restaurant in Adelaide has developed an excellent muntrie chutney conserve which I use, unashamedly, in my recipe for Tomato and Muntrie Salsa. Beautiful served with my recipe for Tasmanian Ocean Trout baked in Paperbark, the salsa is also tantalising with avocado. South Australia is blessed with a range of native mints and peppermints which are marvellous sprinkled over the salsa.

gaultherias (snowberries)

Across on the fine island of Tasmania, the snowberry, *Gaultheria hispida*, graces the embankments of the mountainous countryside. In March, the angelic snow-white crisp berries stand out against the glistening dark leaves of the small hairy shrubs. Gaultheria clusters appear fragile but are in fact quite hardy, able to cope with heat without compromising their delicate flavour. They are delicious when rapidly sautéed in butter with a pinch of brown sugar, then flambed with triple sec and a squirt of lemon juice. The lightly caramelised clusters are a perfect topping to go with crêpes and cider. Like the Tasmanian pepperberry and other cold climate produce, the snowberry stores well in chilled conditions without having to resort to the devastating effect of freezing. A single posy of leaf and berries embellishes any plate when used as a side garnish. The natural appeal of gaultheria genuinely mirrors the freshness and goodness of Tasmania. Gaultheria deserves much more attention from Australian chefs — it's simply beautiful.

Sweet berries & sour fruits recipes

<rosella chutney>

750 g (24 oz) rosella petals, fresh or frozen

500 g (16 oz) Granny Smith apples, peeled and sliced

500 g (16 oz) onions, peeled and sliced

2 chillies, seeded and finely chopped

½ teaspoon cayenne pepper

3 cups (750 ml / 24 fl oz) cider vinegar

1 dessertspoon all spice

4 cloves

2 tablespoons seeded raisins

1 tablespoon salt

750 g (24 oz) sugar

1. Sterilise the jars for the chutney.
2. Cook the first 10 ingredients together for 10 minutes.
3. Add sugar to the mixture, bring to the boil, and cook over a medium heat for 1 hour, stirring regularly.
4. If chutney is chunky enough, bottle immediately in sterilised jars, or cook longer to obtain desired consistency.
5. Serve with kangaroo and emu sausages.

Note: This is based on a well-proven recipe published in 1937 and attributed to 'Mrs C.M.G.' of Oxley, Queensland.

< davidson plum jam >

2 kg (4 lb) of Davidson plums, washed, peeled and seeded

1.75 litres (3 pints / 60 fl oz) water

pectin bag containing pith and seeds of 1 lemon and the core and skin of 1 green apple

2.5 kg (5½ lb) caster sugar (superfine granulated sugar)

3 lemons, juiced and strained

1. Boil fruit in the water for 30 minutes with pectin bag in the mixture, but tied to the jam pan for easy retrieval.
2. Add sugar and lemon juice.
3. Boil, stirring frequently and skimming the surface.
4. Test by sheeting the jam. This is done by placing a small spoonful of jam on a cold saucer and letting it cool. It should wrinkle when pushed with a spoon.
5. Preserve jam in clean sterilised jars.

Note: It is necessary to wear rubber or disposable gloves to wash, peel and seed the fruit as it will stain the skin and the small hairs on the plums may be irritating to some skin types.

Warwick Kent

Davidson plum jam.

Warwick Kent

Glacé fruits: riberry, lemon aspen, rosella.

<glacé riberries or lemon aspens>

1 kg (2 lb) riberries or lemon aspens, fresh or frozen

500 ml (16 fl oz) water

caster sugar (superfine granulated sugar)

2 tablespoons glucose

1. Barely cover fruit with cold water, bring to the boil and cook for 3 minutes.
2. Remove from heat, strain fruit and reserve liquid.
3. Bring liquid back to the boil with 1 cup (220 g / 7 oz) of sugar.
4. Pour resulting syrup over fruit in a clean tray or jar.
5. Next day, strain fruit from the liquid. Reheat liquid with 1 cup (220 g / 7 oz) of sugar and, when boiling, pour immediately over fruit in a fresh clean tray or jar.
6. Repeat this process daily for 7 days. Stop the process for the next 48 hours and then recommence for another 7 days.

Note: The more this process is repeated, the stickier the fruit and syrup become. After 16 or so applications the fruit may be drained and air dried to achieve crystallised fruit. The syrup can be used in a sorbet, as a cordial, or to make fruit jellies.

<tomato and muntrie salsa>

12 roma tomatoes, peeled, deseeded and finely diced
1 teaspoon coriander seeds, coarsely ground
1 large spanish onion (red onion), finely chopped
2 small bunches chives, finely-cut
1 tablespoon sugar
2 tablespoons sweet soy sauce
2 tablespoons cider vinegar
1 teaspoon balsamic vinegar
cracked black pepper to taste
pinch salt
olive oil
250 g (8 oz) Andrew Fielke's muntrie chutney

1. Place tomatoes in a large bowl and sprinkle with coriander.
2. Add spanish onions, chives and sugar.
3. Drizzle the soy all over.
4. Pour over vinegars.
5. Add generous pepper and minimal salt.
6. Pour on enough olive oil to lubricate the salsa.
7. Empty the chutney into the salsa and fold through with a stainless-steel spoon to ensure minimal bruising.
8. Leave to marinate in refrigerator for 30 minutes.

<lemon aspen mayonnaise>

MAKES ABOUT 1 CUP

2 egg yolks
1 tablespoon finely sliced lemon aspens
3 slices spanish onion (red onion)
1 teaspoon French mustard
salt and pepper to taste
1 cup (250 ml / 8 fl oz) grapeseed oil
1 tablespoon lemon juice
1 tablespoon cider vinegar
boiling water

1. Process egg yolks, lemon aspens, onion, mustard, salt and freshly-ground black pepper to taste in a food processor for 5 seconds.
2. With processor running, gradually add oil drop by drop until mixture thickens. Then add remaining oil in a thin steady stream.
3. Add lemon juice, vinegar and enough boiling water (about 1–2 tablespoons) for the desired consistency.

<tamarind butter>

6 native tamarinds (either *Diploglottis campbellii* or *D. australis*)

250 g (8 oz) unsalted butter

1. To preserve the tamarinds, remove the three large segments from their 'cocoon'.
2. Scrape the thin layer of soft flesh from the stone with a penknife.
3. Whisk butter in a food processor on high speed until soft and fluffy.
4. Add the tamarind pulp to the butter and fold in at low speed, scraping the sides of the bowl.
5. Wet the surface of a sheet of greaseproof paper.
6. Place butter mixture in a rough log shape across the width of the sheet.
7. Roll to form a tightly-packed log, approximately 3 cm (1¼ in) in diameter.
8. Compress roll by twisting ends of the paper in opposite directions and store in refrigerator until required.
9. Serve very cold, sliced on grilled fish or steak.

Note: Tamarind butter is excellent. The acidity of the fruit, combined with the creamy butter, is perfectly suited to the cooked flesh of reef fish.

Warwick Kent

Tamarind butter on ice in silver bowl.

Marron, koonacs, gilgies & yabbies

< *cherax* >

In Western Australia, December usually marks the beginning of the 'hunting' season for the world's best-tasting crayfish, the marron *Cherax tenuimanus*. The marron is one of five species of *Cherax* in Western Australia. Belonging to the family of decapods — a large group with prehistoric origins which includes the prawn, shrimp, crab and rock lobster — the marron's natural habitat is the extensive clean-river system extending from Esperance on the southern ocean coast to Geraldton, north of Perth. Increasingly now the marron is being farmed. As a result of finely-tuned aquaculture programs, this delicious freshwater crustacean is available all year round.

marron

Marrons grow large quite rapidly. Two years will see an average adult weigh in at around 200 to 250 g (6½ to 8 oz) with a length of 7.5 cm (3 in), but they have been known to grow to 2 kg (4 lb) and 38.5 cm (15 in) long! Finding a marron like that is exceptional, and the flesh of one that old would be about as succulent as old leather. Marrons are easily recognisable by their deep chestnut, almost black colour, although bright blue specimens are often seen and red ones have even been spotted in the past. The year-old juveniles sport dark markings over their greenish-yellow bodies, while the older ones are brownish, *marron* being French for chestnut. From the tip of the spike on the head, called the rostrum, the marron boasts five ridges or 'keels', as they are called. It also has two spines on top of its tail.

WORLD'S BEST FRESHWATER CRAY

Marrons are exceptional. These clean-river crustaceans are robust and travel well, retaining their firm texture. Marrons harvested from dams are placed in layered, wet hessian with chilled and bagged water — a method replacing the previous one of packing in straw. The layered hessian also reduces the incidence of cannibalism among the

marroning

Catching or selling marrons is strictly controlled. Current regulations require anyone over the age of 13 to apply to the West Australian Department of Fisheries for an inland fisherman's licence to catch wild marrons. A modest fee applies, and the licence only allows you to catch marron in creeks and rivers. Females in berry (having larvae attached to the body) must not be caught, and the bag limit is 20 crayfish a day. Most importantly, no crayfish under the legal size limit of 76 mm must be taken (the measurement is taken from the rostrum on the head to where the carapace meets the start of the tail).

No more than six drop nets (the ones normally used for crab fishing) are permitted and spearguns, harpoons, Hawaiian slings and all other pointed instruments are illegal. Similarly, the use of boats and scuba equipment to catch marrons is also prohibited. Heavy penalties exist for first offenders with increasingly severe penalties for subsequent offences. Furthermore, if undersized crays are caught individual fines apply for each specimen taken. The streams of the dense forests of the south coast are said to be the best for catching the larger crustaceans. Understandably, the marroners of Western Australia are reluctant to disclose their favourite spots. The only hint they are willing to part with is that the best bait for catching wild marrons is fresh meat!

transported marron. When handling marron, care must be exercised to avoid the nippers which are strong and can inflict painful injury. On purchase, the marrons can be stored in their packing for several days in a coolroom or refrigerator.

4 Wheeler / Valerie Martin

Marrons (Cherax tenuimanus) grown for the market by Koogereena Marron Farm, Moonyoonooka, Western Australia.

It is recommended that the marrons are placed in an ice slurry for 20 minutes prior to cooking them. They are cooked by dropping them into rapidly boiling salted water, which can be seasoned with bay leaves, pepper-corns and onions. Ensure that a very large pot is used and only cook a few at a time. For large marrons four to six minutes from boiling point is sufficient cooking time, with a further five minutes standing time required.

Serving marron in their shells is most effective. To remove the tail meat from the cray, scissors are needed to cut through the ribs of the underside. The tail is lifted out, the shell and head are rinsed clean and the intestinal tract removed by pulling from the tail end. The red roe found in the females is particularly tasty and useful in making a coral mayonnaise.

While sauces are great accompaniments, the flesh of marron has a clean natural sweetness that easily stands alone.

koonacs and gilgies

Koonacs (*Cherax plebejus / Cherax glaber*) are generally smaller than marrons, their colour varying from blue-black to a marble-like brownish-black. They are also easy to identify by the four ridges on the back of the head. Koonacs prefer swamps, and although the swamps inevitably dry up in the summer months the koonac can survive for several years under drought conditions by burrowing beneath the crusty surface for moisture. Gilgies (*Cherax quinquecarinatus / Cherax crassimanus*) are brownish-black with blue mottling, sometimes with spots on their claws. They are also good drought survivors, preferring the smaller, less permanent streams. They retreat to a small capped burrow if the water dries up. A licence is not required for the amateur fishing of gilgies and koonacs, but *is* required for marron.

yabbies

The yabby (*Cherax destructor-albidus*) is not indigenous to Western Australia but was introduced to Western Australian dams in the 1940s and '50s. The name *destructor* is particularly appropriate, because they burrow into the walls of irrigation channels. Yabbies are sometimes called 'toe-nippers', as they will mistake a dabbling toe for food.

The yabby is similar to the West Australian koonac (*Cherax plebejus* and *Cherax glaber*), but a yabby is smaller and its claw is narrower and matted with fine hairs.

Yabbies in creeks and farm dams will take on a muddy flavour from their environment. Those cultivated in clean waters are a better quality crayfish, but the flavour still does not compare with that of the marron.

Excessive travelling and handling will traumatise the yabby, and the cooked result can be mushy. A tasty, firm-fleshed yabby results if cooked as soon as possible after capture. This also minimises stress to the creature. At one time yabbies were thrown into boiling water with a handful of salt and cooked for a short time. Today, however, consideration must be given to the ethics of such practices. When cooking any invertebrate, humane preparation is essential.

The cray should be placed in an ice slurry at the ratio of three parts ice to one part water for a minimum of 20 minutes before being boiled. Research has shown that immersion in an ice slurry does not adversely affect the taste or texture of the flesh, but is a humane way to kill the creature before boiling. (These recommendations are from guidelines prepared by the Animal Welfare Advisory Council with input and cooperation from the Restaurant and Catering Association of New South Wales.)

Marron, koonacs, gilgies & yabbies recipes

<summer marron>

1 yellow capsicum (bell pepper), seeded and quartered
2 bunches of rocket (arugula)
6 cooked marron, tails shelled and sliced
olive oil
1 lemon, juiced and strained
pepper
1 carrot, finely julienned and deep fried, for garnish

Prior to cooking, marrons should be chilled for at least 20 minutes in an ice slurry of 3 parts ice and 1 part water, as recommended by the NSW Department of Agriculture and the Animal Welfare Advisory Council.

1. Roast the capsicum in the oven at 250°C (475°F) until charred and blistered. Place in a plastic bag, seal and set aside for 10 minutes.
2. After 10 minutes, peel and deseed capsicum and cut into strips 1 cm (½ in) thick.
3. Place capsicum strips on serving plates and top with rocket leaves.
4. Arrange marron tails over rocket.
5. Drizzle with a little combined olive oil and lemon juice and sprinkle with freshly-ground pepper.
6. Garnish with marron heads and julienned carrot.
7. Serve with Lemon Aspen Mayonnaise (recipe, page 162).

Warwick Kent

Summar marron with salad and lemon aspen mayonnaise.

<yabbies in beer>

- 2 litres (3½ pints / 70 fl oz) draught beer
- 500 ml (16 fl oz) water
- 4 bay or thyme leaves
- 4 tablespoons coarse sea salt
- 1 kg (2 lb) medium to large yabbies

Yabbies are best eaten with fresh bread and butter.

1. Bring beer and water with herbs to the boil.
2. Add salt immediately, followed by the iced-down yabbies.
3. Bring back to the boil and cook for 3 minutes.
4. Drain.

Note: Salt is an important addition to the cooking of freshwater crays. Yabby flesh varies in flavour depending on the source. It can range from bland through to quite muddy. Cultivated yabbies are the most consistent in flavour. Prior to cooking, yabbies should be chilled for at least 20 minutes in an ice slurry of 3 parts ice and 1 part water, as recommended by the NSW Department of Agriculture and the Animal Welfare Advisory Council.

Warwick Kent

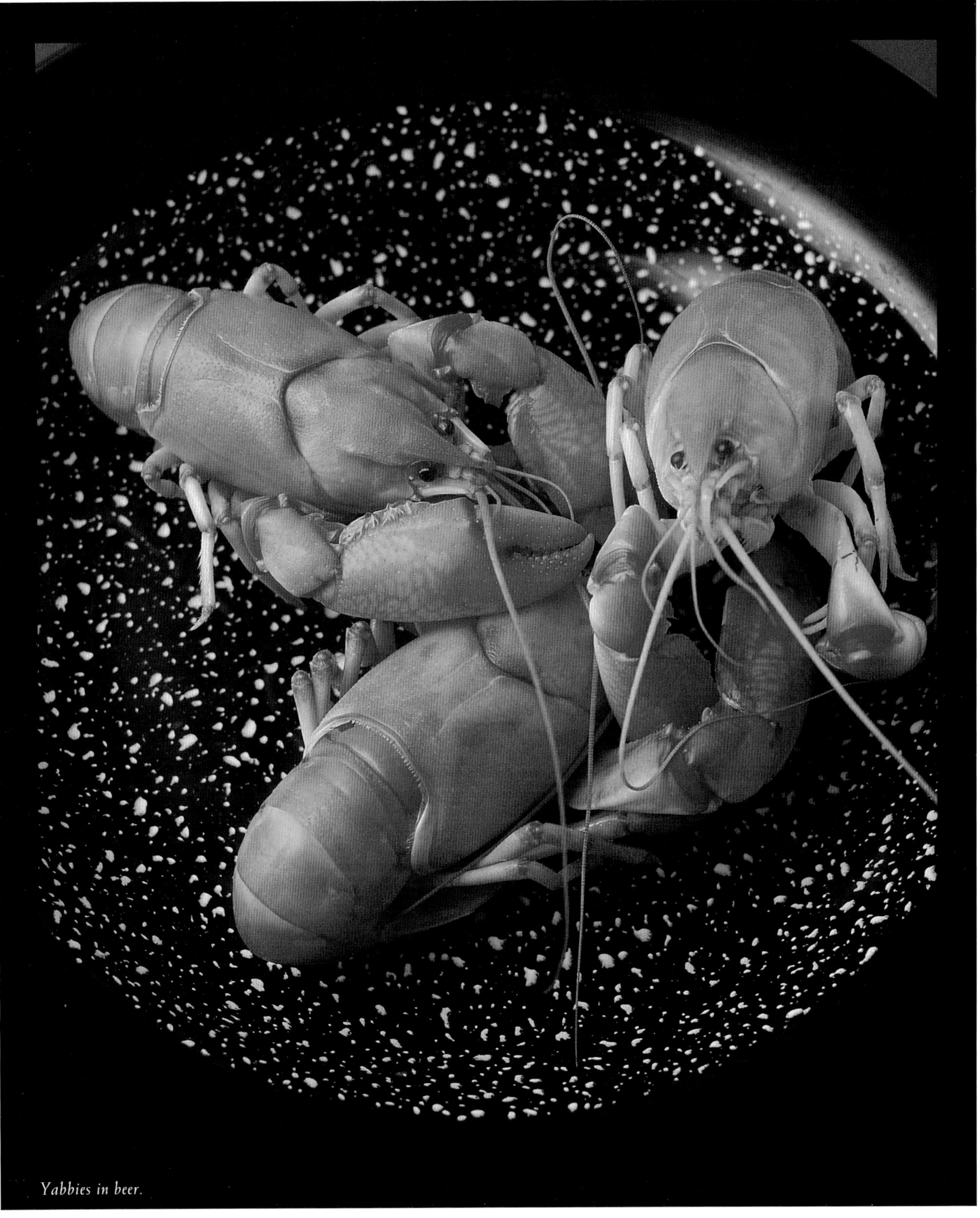

Yabbies in beer.

Yolla, the short-tailed shearwater

< puffinus tenuirostris >

About 9000 years ago the last ice age ended, flooding 15 million hectares of land in southern Australia and creating Bass Strait. Hills and mountains scattered between southern Victoria and north-east Tasmania became islands. These refuges became a coastal breeding home to the short-tailed shearwater.

ancient aquatic bird

The short-tailed shearwater is one of 55 different petrels in the world. Petrels belong to a little-changed ancient group of aquatic birds that have existed for some 64 million years. On take off the bird appears to walk on water as it struggles to gain lift and height, and for this the family received the name petrel for St Peter, who was said also to have walked on water. Their other name 'shearwater' derives from their exploitation of upcurrents and winds deflected from ocean swells on which they bank and slipstream until the lift is exhausted. Yollas live between 15 and 20 years and in a lifetime will fly a staggering 265 000 kilometres (165 000 miles).

The name 'muttonbird' was probably given to the petrel by the settlers of Norfolk Islands who described a slightly different petrel as tasting like mutton. The 'flying sheep', as it was affectionately called, became a very popular food of the new colony. By 1800, this particular muttonbird had deserted Norfolk Island. The indiscriminate taking of adults, chicks and eggs ensured that the bird never came back.

In June and July the icy waters around the Aleutian Islands of the Bering Sea in the Arctic Circle are blanketed by rafts of woolly birds. The Inuit and Aleut people living on the edge of the Bering Sea are well acquainted with the moulted brown feathers floating every year on the icy sea. While they are in the Arctic Circle the ocean provides the birds with a healthy diet of mainly sardines and planktonic life for their non-stop journey back to the nesting sites in Bass Strait. The Arctic people do not harvest the muttonbird as a staple food, possibly because of an abundance of other food choices, such as seals.

flying south

West of the Polynesian Line Island of Palmyra flocks of muttonbirds fly at high speed, six to 30 feet off the water, with as many as 400 000 sighted in a day. The migration, which takes advantage of prevailing winds, causes millions of breeding birds to converge at the end of September on the rookeries of the north-east Tasmanian Furneaux Island group from their northern summer home some 9500 miles away. The birds locate their faithful mate and, if possible, return to their former nest site to clean in preparation for egg laying. The well-worn burrow, an arm's length deep, is lined with vegetation. Two-and-half thousand burrows may be found over one acre of ground. Once the burrows are tidied, each island is deserted once again as the birds prepare to breed.

For the next three weeks intensive feeding takes place. A diet of squid, anchovies and krill fattens the birds in readiness for breeding. In late November, over a two-week period, the entire female population re-descends at dusk to lay their one oval-shaped egg. Moist soil may discolour the smooth white egg brown. The new chicks are born 53 days later.

yolla and the muttonbirders

The Tasmanian Aborigines harvest the young birds from the burrows as they have done for thousands of years. Today this cultural practice is stringently controlled in conjunction with Tasmanian National Parks and Wildlife. Yolla is the name for the muttonbird which is preferred by the Aboriginal community, and yolla farming is a reliable industry based on traditional methods with welcomed financial incentives. By 27 March — the official opening day of muttonbirding — the chicks are two months old and appear downy-grey. The season starts with boats heading to islands east and west of the Bass Strait. The season is short and ends towards the end of April. During this time the Aborigines live on the islands and process thousands of birds before returning to mainland Tasmania.

When the chicks are taken from the burrow they are killed with a skilled swift hand movement which cracks the neck. The muttonbirder then threads the bird by the back of the neck along an oiled pole. The pole, holding about two dozen birds, is carried across the shoulders to the processing huts. Yolla holds a rich oil which is squeezed from the stomach before the birds are plucked.

Traditionally the birds are plucked by scalding in boiling water to remove the rest of the feathers. Then they are cooled, split and gutted. A skun, or skinless bird, is one that has simply been skinned of feathers and fat together. Some plucked birds are later salted. Skun birds are portioned or boned and some are smoked.

Yolla oil has been an important sideline industry to muttonbirding as the quality of the product is high with little or no refining needed. The oil was entered at many international exhibitions of the mid-1800s and, at the Peking Exhibition of 1866, oil from Big Dog Island won awards for quality. In 1870 the Tasmanian railway system was built and large quantities of oil were purchased for lubricating engines and carriages.

FULL FLAVOUR

Traditionally a Tasmanian delicacy, yolla has a strong and distinctive flavour. The fatty birds are rich in monounsaturated and polyunsaturated fats, including fatty acids omega 3 and 6, the essential combination that helps prevent the development of heart disease and strokes. As a wild food, yolla is an excellent source of iron which is more readily absorbed by the body than the iron from cereals. The iron content is calculated at around 50 per cent more than red meat. Analysis shows that yolla also provides more than half the daily requirement of vitamin A for an adult.

In 1993, the Tasmanian Aboriginal Centre officially launched Yolla Promotions, a marketing enterprise aimed at improving the fortune of the industry. The organisation has succeeded in changing the image of the muttonbird as an inferior food source. Many recipes have been developed, and it seems that barbecued yolla is the favourite, especially when the skun bird is marinated in red wine, rosemary and garlic.

Many takeaway food stores in Tasmania sell baked, plucked muttonbirds when in season. Smoking yolla over apple wood or oak shavings is an excellent way to retain the full flavour of the bird, as well as keeping its rosy-pink colour. The smoke flavour accentuates an already delicious food. With a coulibiac — the traditional hot Russian pastry and fish dish — the smoked yolla is a terrific replacement for the expensive salmon which is the usual ingredient.

Warwick Kent

Yolla oil.

Yolla is gourmet food — it is nutritious and never in short supply. The harvesting of yolla by the Tasmanian Aborigines is an important cultural practice with a sound ecological agenda that can only help towards the preservation of the species. The recent transfer of legal title for a number of the Furneaux muttonbirding islands back to Tasmanian Aborigines is a further stepping stone towards eventual full control and management by the Aboriginal community of their traditional industry.

furneaux & flinders

Commanding the *Resolution* on his second expedition, James Cook lost contact with Tobias Furneaux of the *Adventure* in thick fog on 8 February 1773. Following orders laid down for such a mishap, Furneaux sailed east to New Zealand to rejoin Cook three months later. In more favourable conditions, Furneaux may have chartered the strait of water that Matthew Flinders was to later name in honour of his high-spirited partner George Bass.

Flinders was commissioned by Governor Hunter to sail south in the *Norfolk* to prove that a passage of water existed between the southern tip of Victoria and Van Diemen's Land. The existence of the strait was considered probable after the wrecking of the *Sydney Cove* on Preservation Island at midnight on 7 February 1797, and the subsequent 600-kilometre (370 miles) horror trek for help made by some of the ship's crew.

Starting off by longboat, which was itself wrecked later, 17 crewmen unwittingly crossed the strait. Only three members of the party survived to reach Sydney and seek help for those still on Preservation Island. Those who awaited rescue were the first Europeans recorded as dining on muttonbird, which they used to supplement their meagre rice ration.

When Flinders finally sailed through the strait with Bass, he witnessed the phenomena of millions of short-tailed shearwaters converging on the Bass Strait Islands. He recorded that, 'They were 50 to 80 yards in depth and 300 yards or more in breadth'.

From that quick observation, Flinders estimated that it would take 75 750 000 burrows to house the estimated 150 000 000 birds that flew over the *Norfolk* in just an hour and a half. And this, he said, was only one flock.

< yolla savoury dip >

1. Bake eggplant in a 200°C (400°F) oven for approximately 45 minutes. Cool and split open.
2. Shred the yolla finely using a food processor and set aside.
3. With the beater at high speed, whip the cream cheese and lemon juice to a smooth 'cream'.
4. Purée the eggplant flesh in the food processor.
5. Combine the yolla, eggplant and the cream cheese mixtures in the food processor, season with white pepper. Allow to stand 1 hour before serving.
6. Serve with melba toast.

1 medium-sized eggplant (aubergine)

200 g (6½ oz) smoked yolla

250 g (8 oz) cream cheese

4 large lemons, squeezed and strained

white pepper

melba toast (made from thinly sliced bread baked at 150°C / 300°F for 4–5 minutes, or until crisp but not coloured)

<smoked yolla coulibiac>

PROVER FOR THE DOUGH

260 ml (8½ fl oz) warm milk

a little sugar

1 sachet of dry yeast

THE DOUGH

500 g (16 oz) plain flour (all-purpose flour)

1 teaspoon sea salt

2 large eggs

2 teaspoons extra virgin olive oil

EXTRA

1 egg yolk for sealing

1 beaten egg yolk with a little milk to paint the dough for colour

THE FILLING

500 g (16 oz) smoked yolla, shredded

100 g (3½ oz) whipped cream cheese

250 g (8 oz) onions, finely chopped sautéed

250 g (8 oz) small leeks, thinly sliced

4 tablespoons chives, finely-chopped

4 mushrooms, finely chopped

4 hard-boiled eggs, shredded

1 tablespoon chopped dill

1 tablespoon ground coriander seeds

2 tablespoons cream sherry

a good pinch of freshly-ground black pepper

50 g (1½ oz) butter

Coulibiac is a hot Russian *pâté en croute* normally made with Arctic salmon or fowl. Traditionally coulibiac is served with melted butter. It is delicious cold and makes a tasty picnic treat.

1. Make prover by adding the warm milk and sugar to the dry yeast. Allow to stand in a warm place for 20 minutes.
2. Make a well of the sifted flour and salt. Add the prover, eggs and oil.
3. Work the dough to bread consistency.
4. Place the dough in a greased warm bowl. Cover with a tea towel and leave to double in size (90 minutes).
5. Knock the dough back and let prove for another hour in a warm place.
6. Mix all the filling ingredients together while the dough is proving.
7. When the dough has proved, turn it onto a floured board and knead a little.
8. Roll out the dough in a oval shape onto a floured tea towel.
9. Place the filling onto the dough, slightly off centre.
10. Paint the edges of the dough with egg yolk.
11. Fold the ends in and roll to totally seal.
12. Place on greased tray, seams down, and prove for another hour out of cold draughts.
13. Brush the loaf with a beaten egg yolk and milk; prick three sets of ventilation holes with a fork.
14. Bake in a preheated oven at 200°C (400 °F) for approximately 35 minutes.
15. Turn out onto wire rack.

4 Wheeler/Warwick Kent

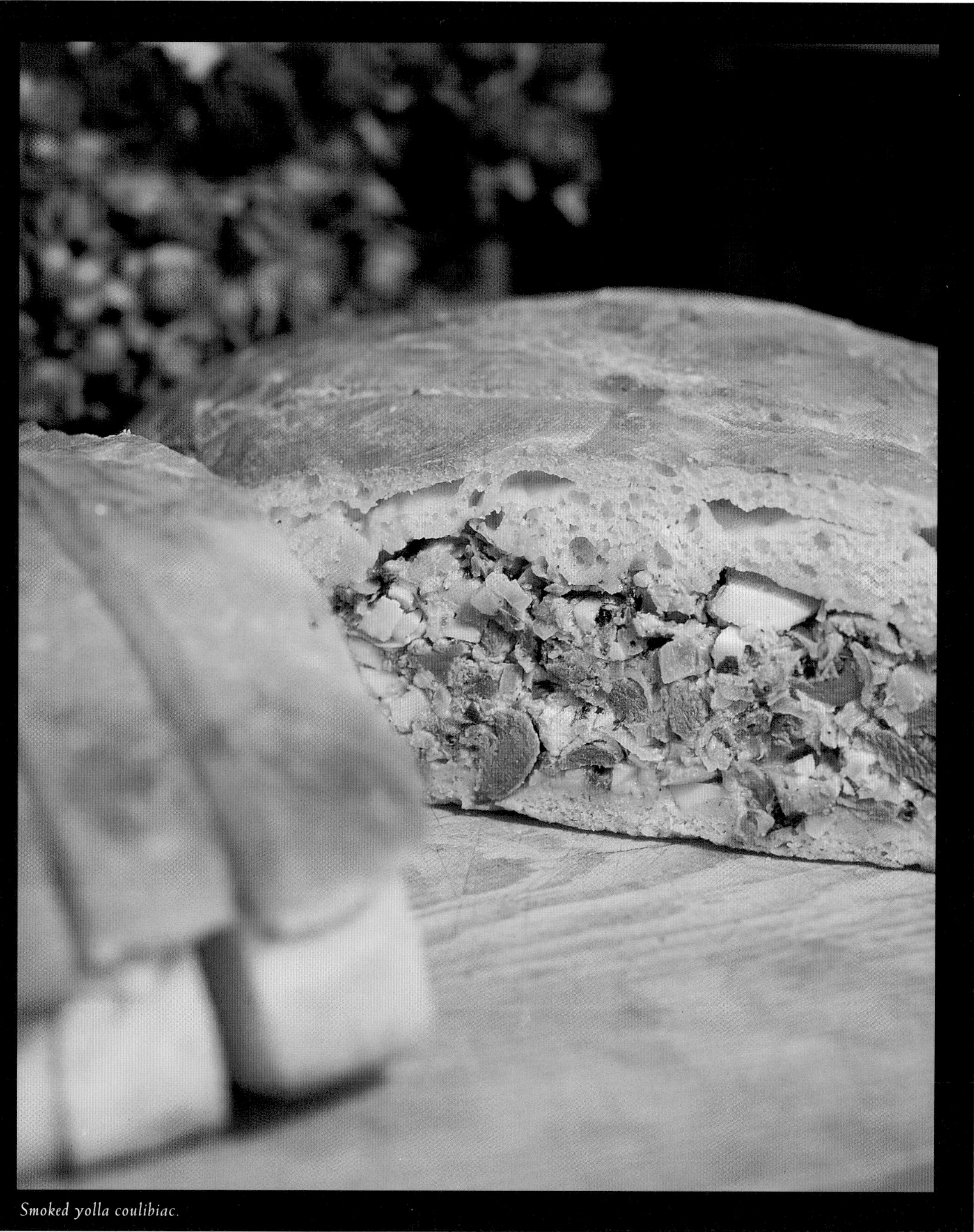

Smoked yolla coulibiac.

<smoked yolla and trout mousse>

- 100 g (3½ oz) smoked yolla
- 250 ml (8 fl oz) milk
- 100 g (3½ oz) smoked trout
- 2 whole eggs
- 5 egg yolks
- 250 ml (8 fl oz) fresh cream
- ½ teaspoon finely ground sassafras leaves (*Atherosperma moschatum*)
- 50 g (1¾ oz) butter

1. Preheat oven to 200°C (400°F).
2. Place the yolla and half the milk in a blender and render to a paste.
3. Cut the smoked trout into thin strips.
4. In a bowl, mix the yolla with whole eggs, yolks, cream, remaining milk and sassafras.
5. Strain the mixture through a fine sieve.
6. Grease 10 small ramekins with butter. Divide the smoked trout equally between the ramekins and arrange on the base of each.
7. Place ramekins in a baking tray filled with boiling water.
8. Place in oven, reduce temperature to 170°C (340°F), and bake for 20 minutes or until mixture is set.
9. Serve with steamed asparagus and, if desired, a lime hollandaise.

<barbecued yolla>

- 2 skun birds
- olive oil

MARINADE

- 500 ml (16 fl oz) burgundy wine
- 2 tablespoons rosemary, finely chopped
- 5 small hot chillies, seeded and cut into thin strips
- 1 tablespoon ground coriander seeds
- 5 cloves garlic, minced

1. Marinate sectioned birds for 36 hours.
2. Drain birds on a wire rack for 1 hour.
3. Cover birds with olive oil 2 hours before cooking.
4. Cook on medium-hot barbecue for 3–5 minutes.

Warwick Kent

Barbecued yolla.

Oysters, periwinkles & mussels

Gathering the shellfish which greatly contributed to the daily food requirement was the job of the Aboriginal women, with the men assisting with their collection at times of greatest dependence, when other food sources were seasonally poor or unavailable. John Hunter, who later became Governor of the colony, observed in the early days of Sydney that men dived for shellfish which were hastily opened on tidal rock ledges.

Collecting oysters from the mangroves in northern New South Wales.

oysters

The Sydney rock oyster (*Saccostrea commercialis*) is considered a gourmet item and is the basis of an industry employing 3000 people in New South Wales. Native to Japan, the Pacific oyster (*Crassostrea gigas*) threatens the possible displacement of the Sydney rock oyster from the oyster bed as well as the table. The industry is taking measures to prevent this from happening in the Sydney region where, in 1985, the Pacific oyster was declared a noxious fish. In other areas, like Tasmania, Victoria and South Australia, the Pacific oyster is the centre of a flourishing industry. Oysters from Jervis Bay in New South Wales, while flatter, creamier and more stubbornly attracted to the shell than both Sydney and Pacific oysters, also provide excellent eating.

Oysters are bivalve molluscs found between tidal levels or in shallow waters, and can live a long life of up to 20 years. They are ready for the table after two to three years — in the case of the Sydney rock oysters — and after only ten months to two years in the case of the Pacific variety. Monitoring water quality for degrees of bacterial contamination, particularly after periods of heavy rain, is a method practised to ensure consistent oyster quality. As oysters are filter feeders, great care is taken by the Oyster Growers industry to ensure that all oysters are subject to purification processing in sterilised seawater, which is filtered through the mollusc at the rate of 12 litres an hour.

periwinkles

In the coastline zone above the barnacle band, which is only occasionally reached by high tides, live the univalve periwinkles (*Ausbrocochlea spp*). Huddling together to prevent themselves drying out in the exposed air, these marine snails survive by grazing on algae. Growing to 2 cm at their widest point, they are easily recognised by their strong cone-shaped shell which protects them from predators. The shell is patterned with circling wavy lines of grey and black, which give them their alternative name, wavy turbo. Periwinkles, although edible, have never attained the prestige of the oyster or the mussel. Often used as bait, the periwinkle gained some use during World War Two as a pet-food substitute when meat was scarce.

The periwinkle of Tasmania (*Subninella undulata*) has had a measure of success on the shellfish market. Harvested by commercial divers from subtidal reefs and platforms, catch rates of 20 to 50 kilograms an hour are achievable, with some claims of up to 100 kilograms an hour. The industry is directing its catch to restaurants as a ready-to-use, cook-in-the-shell frozen product, as well as exporting live periwinkles to mainland fish markets, where they are well received.

mussels

Mussels (*Mytilus planulatus*) are bivalves like the oyster and are very good eating. They vary from brown to purple-black and can be found clustered on mooring ropes and

midden calendars

Shellfish are a significant component in the diet of indigenous peoples all around Australia, in freshwater locations as well as coastal and estuarine regions. Occasional reliance on shellfish by some groups is counterpointed by seasonal gorging and even continuous feasting by others. Middens, the heaped shell remains of the catch, reflect the immense quantity of shellfish gathered and demonstrate the level of dependence upon this highly-valued food source. Middens also give confirmation of a preference for particular shellfish types. At Weipa on Cape York in Queensland, for example, the middens predominantly contain cockle shells, while at the Clarence River in New South Wales, the remains are almost exclusively oysters. At Gymea Bay near Sydney the shells are varied, including Sydney rock oysters or *patanga*, cockles or *warabi*, mussels and periwinkles. Oysters were often opened on site and eaten raw; however, most shellfish were roasted or broiled over hot coals.

Ironically, just as it was the work of Aboriginal women to gather the shellfish to support the dietary needs of the tribe, the collection of midden shells for lime production was the assigned task of the women convicts of the penal settlement. The collected shells were taken to Limeburners Point (now Bennelong Point where the Sydney Opera House stands) to be converted into Sydney's first building mortar. Despite the immensity of the middens, settlers lamented the fact that only a quarter of the required lime could be produced by this method. Hence the search for limestone began.

lines and wharves and jetty piles, as well as tidal rock ledges in the cooler waters below 32 degrees latitude. Freshwater mussels (*velesunio sp.*) are found in muddy streams and can be 'fished' for by feeling about with the feet — taking care to avoid the toe-nipping yabbies that live in the same environment.

exceptional divers

George Robinson, the government-appointed investigator of Aboriginal populations in Tasmania, noted in his 1832 journals that Aboriginal women were expert divers and swimmers. Although most shellfish can be gathered at low tide from easily-accessible rock platforms, the women stayed underwater for alarmingly long periods of time to resurface with crayfish, abalone and crabs, as well as mussels and periwinkles, which they put into small woven bags slung around their necks.

Aboriginal people of Tasmania had a greater dependence on shellfish than indigenous mainlanders, for fish with scales was to them a strict taboo. Food taboos often exist to protect a food source, for example, at particular times such as breeding seasons, or to limit a

4 Wheeler/Warwick Kent

Removing the radula from periwinkles.

food's availability to the majority of the population to prevent its overexploitation. George Robinson remarked that the taboo on scaled fish was absolute and that scaled fish even evoked fear in one tribe. James Cook's presentation of an elephant fish to the Tasmanian Aborigines he encountered could easily have been considered a great offence. Their firm refusal of the gift of 'food' surprised Cook and his crew. There is midden evidence from one location in Little Swanport, Tasmania that scaled fish *were* once included in the diet, but the fish bones were located at a midden level dated between 4750 and 3550 years ago.

reliable food item

Today the shellfish industry of Australia is supplying a top-quality product to an appreciative market. While shellfish can still be found in tidal areas for the taking, in a world conscious of pollution commercial producers strive to supply uncontaminated oysters, mussels and periwinkles that can be consumed without the worry often associated with the wild-harvested varieties. Freshly-shucked oysters are the best eating, especially during the summer months when the oyster is at its largest and creamiest, filling the shell and almost popping up when it is opened. As spawning occurs after rain and changes in temperature, the winter months tend to produce an leaner oyster. With the conditions of each river being so different, it is possible to obtain high-quality oysters all year round.

In Sydney, the riberry is also in season during the summer months, and the flavour of this clove lillipilli is wonderfully refreshing with Sydney rock oysters served with a little smoked salmon. Lemon-scented backhousia leaves infused into white-wine vinegar, cooled and coupled with finely-chopped purple onion and fresh chives provide the acid that marries so well with oysters. One way to shuck and eat cooked oysters is to place them unopened onto hot coals. This will fire them quickly in the shell and causes the lid to spring open. When baking oysters in an oven, paperbark placed over the shucked oysters will impart a pleasantly subtle mushroom-smoked flavour.

Mussels, unlike oysters, *must* be cooked. Only closed shells should be used as only dead mussels stay open. Mussels tend to disgorge liquid in storage; this juice must be drained and the mussels rinsed if the shellfish are to be kept over a few days. If this simple step is not taken, some of the mussels will quickly die and putrify the others. To prepare for cooking, the beard or byssus (used as an anchor) is removed by twisting and tugging. Mussels readily take on flavours in their cooking. They can be poached in wine with herbs and other ingredients, or wok-fried as intense heat is the key to a good mussel. The soft membrane or mantle may be either white or orange. The best mussels that I have eaten were wild mussels from Eden, New South Wales. These very large, free-ranging bivalves were dived for, unlike the cultivated mussels which are grown on artificial stakes or mooring ropes.

Oysters, periwinkles & mussels recipes

<baked oysters under paperbark>

1 dozen oysters, opened and washed in iced, salted water

coarse rock salt, for placing the oysters on tray

1 roll paperbark

DIPPING SAUCE

Lemon-scented Myrtle Vinegar (recipe, page 130)

spanish onion (red onion), finely chopped

chives

dash of balsamic vinegar

1. Place clean oysters on rock salt.
2. Cover the oysters with paperbark.
3. Microwave oysters on high for 30 seconds.
4. Make accompanying dipping sauce by combining the ingredients.

< tasmanian garlic periwinkles >

2 kg (4 lb) periwinkles in shells

plenty of water, with a generous amount of sea salt for cooking periwinkles

THE SAUCE

1 onion, finely chopped

3 cloves garlic, minced

½ teaspoon black pepper

2 tablespoons basil, finely chopped

2 tablespoons (50 g / 1¾ oz) butter

6 ripe roma tomatoes, skinned, peeled and deseeded

3 tablespoons tomato paste

60 ml (2 fl oz) brandy

THE LIDS

1 loaf white, sliced sandwich bread

2 cloves garlic, minced

250 g (8 oz) butter, melted

Snail dishes are required for this recipe. These plates are fitted with either 6 or 12 egg-cup-shaped indentions which are perfect for sealing the sea snails and sauce under a flavoured crouton cap.

1. Wash periwinkles in clean water.
2. Drop periwinkles in boiling salted water. Cover with a lid.
3. Bring back to the boil and cook for 3 minutes without the lid, then strain.
4. While still hot, pull the periwinkle out of the shell with a two-pronged fork or a sharp skewer.
5. With a sharp pair of scissors, cut off ¾ of the radula (the periwinkle's foot).
6. Make the tomato sauce by frying the onions, garlic, pepper and basil in butter with the tomatoes, tomato paste and brandy. Cook for 15 minutes in oven at 200°C (400°F) and then purée and strain. Season with salt if desired.
7. Place a teaspoon of tomato mixture in each cup and then put in periwinkle.
8. Cut croutons to a size slightly over that of the cup rims.
9. Dip croutons in melted butter and spread the underside with minced garlic. Place over cup.
10. Bake at 200°C (400°F) for 6 to 8 minutes. Cool for 5 minutes before serving.
11. Pushing a fork into the side of the crouton and scooping will cause the crouton to pivot and collect the periwinkle and sauce with it.

Caution: The contents of the cups will be extremely hot and the sauce can scald.

Warwick Kent

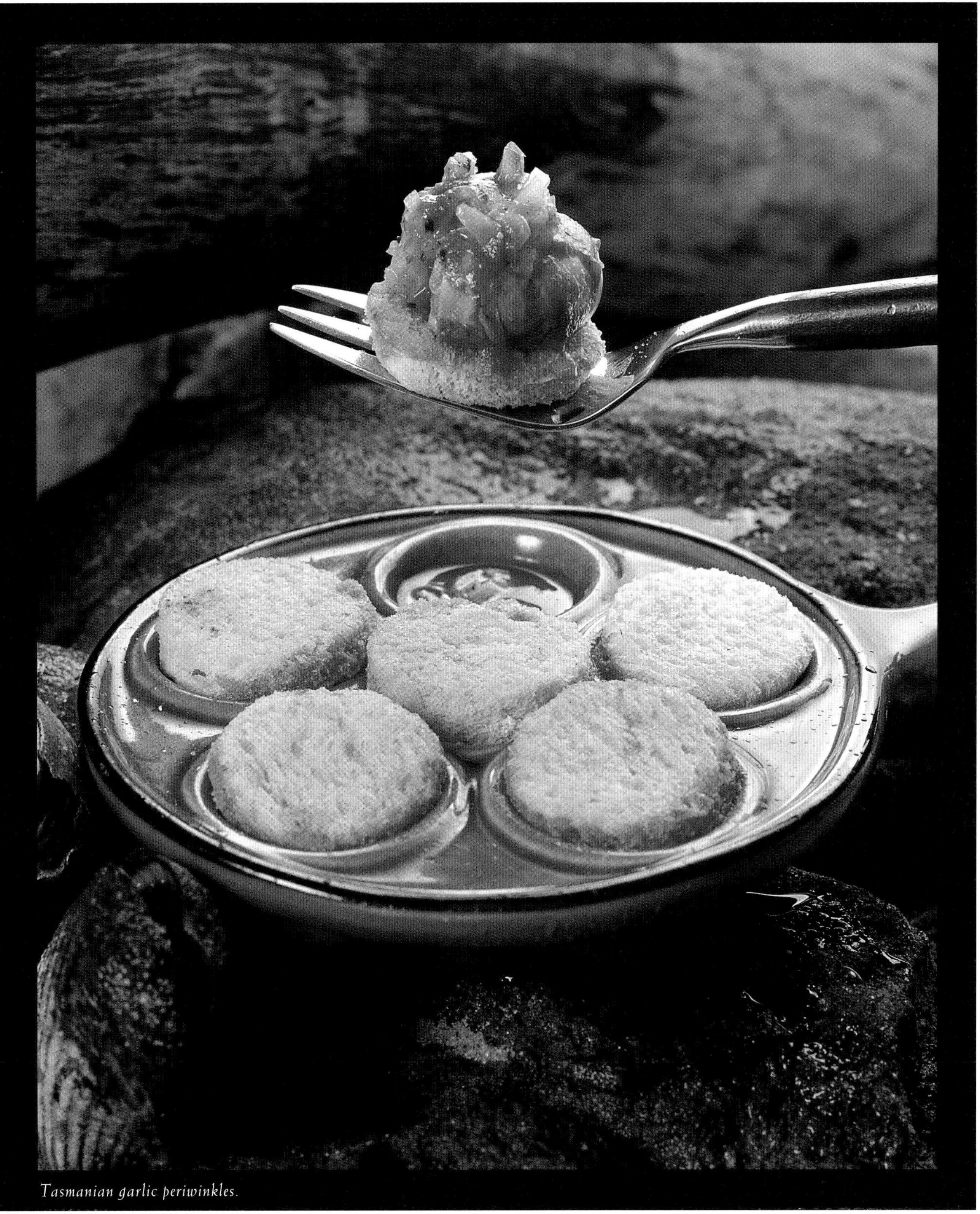

Tasmanian garlic periwinkles.

<broiled mussels and sassafras>

2 kg (4 lb) mussels, washed and bearded

1 spanish onion (red onion), chopped

2 cloves garlic, sliced

5 hot chillies, seeded and ringed

1 teaspoon dried, ground sassafras leaf (*Atherosperma moschatum*)

1 cup (250 ml / 8 fl oz) riesling or other sweet white wine

Delicious with a slice of *pasta dura* bread soaked in extra virgin olive oil and sizzled on a hot barbecue plate to soak up the juices.

1. Heat heavy-based pan for 5 minutes on high heat.
2. Pour enough olive oil in to cover bottom of pan. Oil should smoke on contact.
3. Immediately pour the mussels into the pan, followed by onion, chillies, garlic and sassafras.
4. Toss quickly, cover with a tight lid and cook for 3 minutes.
5. Pour in white wine, toss and cook further 2 minutes and serve with chopped fresh continental parsley.

<oysters with riberry relish>

250 g (8 oz) riberries

1 green apple, peeled and shredded

100 ml (3½ fl oz) white-wine vinegar

100 ml (3½ fl oz) lemon juice

50 g (2 oz) white sugar

2 cloves

The acidity of the riberry takes to sweetening quite well. When vinegar is added too, the riberry becomes infinitely suited to the plump richness of summer oysters.

1. Place ingredients in a stainless-steel saucepan and stir well.
2. Cook for 15 minutes over medium heat, stirring occasionally.
3. Remove cloves.
4. Blend the mixture at high speed.
5. Strain mixture through fine mesh, using a wooden spoon to push it through.
6. Refrigerate the relish well before dolloping a small amount on the hinge quarter of the oyster.
7. Garnish oysters with a small strip of smoked trout.

Oysters with riberry relish.

4 Wheeler/Warwick Kent

billy-goat plum

< *terminalia ferdinandiana* >

In 1980, the Australian Armed Forces began to display a keen interest in the viability and value of wild foods, survival in the bush being vital to army personnel in the unlikely event of an invasion. In the Top End, Major Les Hiddins (also known as 'The Bushtucker Man') collected samples of wild foods for study at the Materials Research Laboratory at Scottsdale, Tasmania. While exploring (mostly off-road) he mapped and referenced many species of nuts, fruits and berries for evaluation. One of the Major's finds raised the immediate attention of his colleagues at Scottsdale: a green plum *Terminalia ferdinandiana* **which tests revealed as having an unusually high concentration of vitamin C.**

Department of Defence, Defence Science and Technology Organisation Scottsdale, Tasmania.

Billy-goat plums at the defence laboratories where the fruit was first analysed.

major find

Les Hiddins, still at large and 4-wheeling around the Alice, was ordered to back-track almost 1000 miles to collect more of the green plum for the astonished analyst. Conclusive testing at the University of Sydney recorded a profile of 4.8 to 5.2 per cent of ascorbic acid (vitamin C), with folic acid (vitamin B complex) also present.

Brian Woods in the Northern Territory has a keen interest in the plum and has completed his Masters degree on the commercial potential of this remarkable fruit. He concedes that some trees do produce fruit that achieve a level of 5.9 per cent of vitamin C. These extraordinary fruits are up to 120 times higher in vitamin C than oranges, and they supersede the acerola cherry (*Malpithia punicifloia*), a native of West Indies, as the highest-yielding source of the vitamin known.

The green plum — unofficially named by Les Hiddins as the kakadu plum — has many common names. *Murunga* is one of at least 20 local Aboriginal names; billy-goat plum, salty plum and capricorn plum are among the names given to the plum by wild-food enthusiasts.

The research associated with the billy-goat plum has brought about a timely recognition of Aboriginal foods and marks the beginning of a genuine interest in Australian native foods.

billy-goat face

This deciduous tree is common in northern Australia and proliferates freely in the vast area between Katherine in the Northern Territory and Broome in the west. It is a familiar tree among the northern flora, with most trees averaging six to eight metres (20 to 27 feet) high. A good tree of 10 metres (32 feet) or higher can yield large amounts of fruit — up to 40 to 50 kilograms (88 to 110 pounds) each. Brian Woods has measured his tallest tree at 10.5 metres (34 feet) and has estimated the yield of another very large tree at around 80 kilograms (176 pounds). The small, goat-faced, waxy fruit resembles a green olive to touch and is related to the Indian almond (*Terminalia catappa*). An excellent specimen of a large *Terminalia ferindandiana* tree exists at Nourlangie Rock, near the bus terminal, in Kakadu National Park.

The fruit hold throughout the extremely dry months of May, June and July. These dry months, known to the Aborigines of Arnhem Land as *Dharratharra mirri*, are a time of cool nights, misty mornings, cracked ground and burnt dry grass — a time when the billy-goat plum is the only fruit left on the trees, an important fact for survival.

world interest

The discovery of the world's greatest vitamin C source met with enormous publicity and was heralded as a major find with excellent commercial prospects. Following a front-page news item in the *Wall Street Journal*, a short-lived American company began looking for a suitable location in the United States to grow the plum ahead of the Australians. The company, known as Terminalia Inc, experimented with freeze-dried products to be used in general food applications. The company folded quickly and their results are either lost or classified. The European interest in

Terminalia ferdinandiana extends to natural therapies and pharmaceutical research with French, German and Swiss companies having published articles about this Australian fruit. The Australian branch of a large, overseas, pharmaceutical manufacturing company has experimented with the plum as a flavouring for food. Unfortunately this excellent work has been suspended.

sensitive to heat and sugar

My first taste experience of this pleasantly sour, fibrous little plum impressed me. The sample was fresh fruit and reminded me of English gooseberries. The first impression was the best — frozen samples were never as good. Water lost through thawing accentuates the fibrous nature of the plum and the interesting sour tang diminishes. Early attempts to cook the fruit produced a poor result. Excessive heat can make the plum taste dry and acquire an unpleasant ferrous aftertaste. Scalding the fruit and pickling them like olives or gherkins with garlic, chillies, lime or backhousia leaves is the best way to use the plums, apart from eating them fresh. As an accompaniment to smoked meats or fish they are superb.

Surprisingly, sugar reacts poorly with the plum, although Juleigh and Ian Robbins, the Victorian bush food epicureans, produce an excellent 'Kakadu Plum Jelly' using some sugar. The Robbins have had their product tested and report that a significant amount of the vitamin C is still present even after cooking. The jelly goes particularly well with roast duck and is a great fruit glaze with the Illawarra Plum and Nutmeal Tart. The fibrous nature of the fruit is its only drawback; however, an Australian-developed machine can remove the flesh from the pit successfully. This gives the billy-goat plum further possibilities. This easily-carried medicine food, best enjoyed as a fresh fruit, is a thirst quencher with a really long-lasting chew.

medicinal plum

Food biologists have researched the role of the plum in traditional Aboriginal medicine. The fruit is known to be a good tonic and health restorative. Only ripe fruit that can be shaken from the tree is used. Some communities not only use the plum, but also the bark, which is soaked and made into a sticky solution for the treatment of skin complaints, backache, and sore feet. The flavourless gum, which is eaten, has been analysed as a valuable source of soluble fibre. Current research focuses not only on the fruit itself, but also on ways in which to cultivate, harvest, and process this abundant vitamin source. The future may lie in genetic engineering to isolate and copy the genes responsible for the high levels of natural vitamin C and introduce that gene into other plants such as peaches and plums. Regrettably, it will take an enormous amount of expensive research to identify the gene responsible for the vitamin C.

billy-goat plum recipes

<northern delights>

300 g (10 oz) billy-goat plums, flesh sliced off stone with very sharp blade

500 g (16 oz) granulated sugar

150 ml (5 fl oz) water

1 lemon, juiced and strained, reserved rind cut into thin strips

30 g (1 oz) powdered gelatine

150 ml (5 fl oz) hot water

2 tablespoons icing sugar mixture, sieved

1. Drop the plum flesh into a juice extractor; reserve juice.
2. Dissolve the sugar in 150 ml (5 fl oz) water on medium heat.
3. Add lemon juice, plum juice and lemon rind.
4. Bring the solution to the boil and simmer for 20 minutes.
5. Sprinkle gelatine over hot water and allow to dissolve.
6. Add the gelatine to the syrup and bring to the boil, stirring continuously for 15 minutes.
7. Strain the liquid into a wet, shallow baking tray and set in a cool place for 24 hours.
8. Turn out slab, cut to desired size and roll in sugar mixture.

Warwick Kent

Northern delights.

<pickled billy-goat plums>

- 500 ml (16 fl oz) white-wine vinegar
- 350 g (11 oz) billy-goat plums, thawed or fresh
- 8 sprigs of thyme (fresh or dry)
- 2–3 lemon-scented myrtle leaves
- 2 tablespoons black or white peppercorns
- 1 tablespoon coarse salt
- 2 tablespoons caster sugar (superfine granulated sugar) to soften the bite of the vinegar
- 1.5 litres (4¾ pints / 55 fl oz) boiling water

Pickling is an ancient way of preserving foods. The method used in this recipe is very simple. There are many variations of pickling brines, the dominant ingredient always being vinegar. For this recipe you will need a strainer and sterilised, sealable jars. The minimum preserving time is 3 weeks and the maximum 12 months plus.

1. Sterilise jars and lids in boiling water and keep submerged until required.
2. Bring water to the boil for first scalding.
3. Bring vinegar, salt and sugar to just below boiling point.
4. Throw washed plums into boiling water and turn the heat off immediately.
5. Leave the plums in the water for approximately 3 minutes.
6. Transfer the plums to the jar/s, spiking the preserve with thyme, lemon-scented myrtle leaves and peppercorns.
7. For the second scalding, pour boiling vinegar over the plums. Remove any air bubbles with a sterilised spoon.
8. Seal and store in the refrigerator until ready for use.
9. Serve with Smoked Emu (recipe, page 75).

Warwick Kent

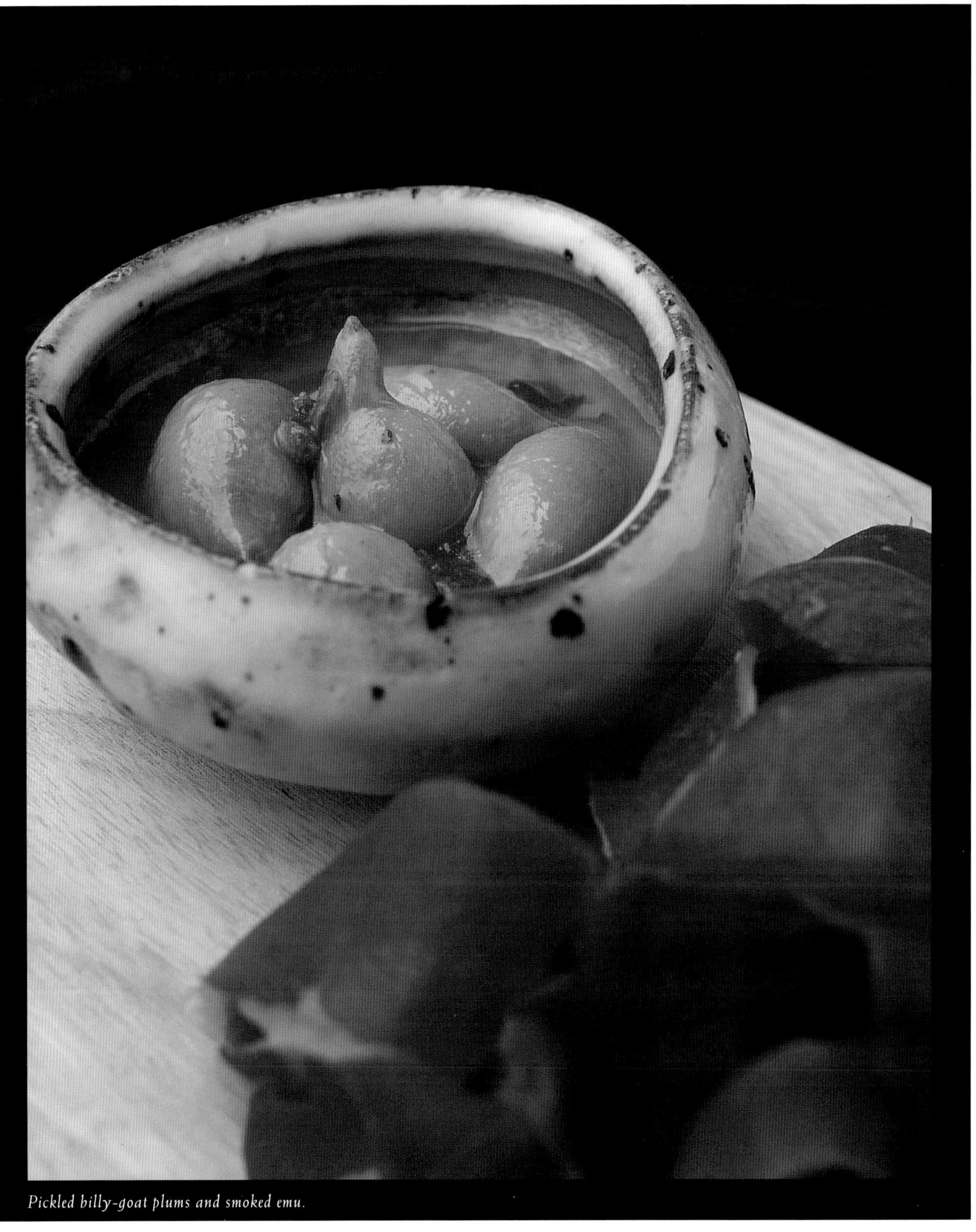

Pickled billy-goat plums and smoked emu.

Wattleseed

< acacia species >

I can say with certainty that the flavour of wattleseed will become a world favourite, as have the flavours of vanilla and chocolate. The native wattle will benefit the farmer, the soils and the economy. It is a commodity of great value to Australia if properly and seriously considered. Fast growing and high yielding, dry-zone acacias will allow an industry to develop within a reasonably short time frame without needing to rely on long-term wild harvesting. Wattleseed is a reliable and abundant drought-resistant crop. When other crops wilt during Australia's unforgiving and unpredictable dry spells, it is imperative to back a native species suited to the vast, arid environment.

seeds, green & dried

Warwick Kent

Roasted wattleseed (*Acacia victoriae*).

Across the vast dry zones of outback Australia hundreds of *Acacia* species grow, some providing gum, seeds, grubs and a timber often used for musical instruments. Mulga wood is also used for artefacts and weapons. At least 49 species are consumed by Central Australian Aborigines, who eat the seeds green like peas, or dried and ground.

The bulk of the acacia seeds are primarily collected by skilled women of outback communities. Collecting the seed and processing it is a time-consuming and tedious affair. Branches heavily laden with the green pods are carried back to a central area where grass fires are built under them. The heat action opens the pods easily, exposing the unripe seeds which are eaten immediately. When dry seeds are harvested, the branches are stripped of pods and collected traditionally in wooden coolamons, after which the women return home to thresh and winnow. Threshing is carried out on blankets — the pods beaten open with wooden clubs, and the seeds falling to the bottom of the heap allowing the pods and detritus to be removed from the top.

Once threshing has finished, winnowing or 'yandying' is important to clean out smaller fragments of pod, dirt and grit. Winnowing is achieved by placing the seed on a tray and using wind assistance to blow the debris away while the seed is bounced up and down. Bouncing is followed by a series of rolling actions which cause further separation. 'Parching' may then follow for harder seeds — the seeds are mixed with hot ashes, coals and soil to soften their hard casing. Other hard-cased seeds are processed by pounding, a handful at a time, on a large flat stone using a round hammer stone — and again winnowing the result.

Warwick Kent

Grinding stone with wattleseeds.

Grinding is the last step before the dried seed can be used. The seed is mixed with a trickle of water on the grindstone and the resulting paste is collected in a coolamon. For a finer mill the paste is ground a second time. The final product is usually eaten raw but can also be used in bread.

shared group

Apart from the fantastic flavour, wattle is nutritionally beneficial. Charged with an average of 32 per cent fibre, 26 per cent carbohydrate, 23 per cent protein and 9 per cent fat, wattleseed is a complete food source long exploited by Aboriginal people. Edible polyunsaturated oils with mono-unsaturated fatty acids are also derived from certain seeds and food analysts have now revealed that a number of acacias are low glycaemic-index foods. Such foods allow starch to be slowly released giving a gradual and sustained rise in blood sugars.

premium blend

In Australia, many techniques for roasting wattleseed have been tried, the first with disastrous results. The bulk of the original investment became tainted with ginger due to negligence, and unattractive packaging further diminished the product's appeal. Since these early days, new methods have been explored and new technologies applied. Gundabluey Bushfoods of Sydney, the company specialising in wattleseed, developed a unique process in 1995 that achieved consistent results and a variety of roasts, vital for different culinary applications.

The essential flavour of wattle is only released when cooked with water, the aroma reflecting the taste. The short-lived original 'wattleseed essence' manufactured at Rowntrees, The Australian Restaurant was too thin and restricted to too few applications. 'Gundabluey' Mud is now the preferred flavouring method in cooking, as the

Tim Low

Acacia victoriae pods on tree, Broken Hill, New South Wales.

gundabluey

As a food plant, the seeds of a few *Acacia* species are very palatable and highly nutritious. This has led to my interest in the seeds of two particular dry-zone species: *Acacia victoriae* and *Acacia murrayana*. This food is manna from heaven. Once the seed is cleaned and roasted it can be ground and brewed in the same way as coffee. My first taste for wattle began with Vic Cherikoff. Sometime in 1986 Cherikoff had given me a sample of *Acacia victoriae* to experiment with. The plastic bottle came three-quarters filled with a strange brown grit with a peculiar aroma. After a few very unsuccessful trials using the wattle as a spice or seasoning, I did not hold much hope for its future.

The last resort was to be an extraction by way of espresso. The aroma exuded by brewing was followed by an anxious tasting. The result was quickly interpreted as a gastronomic find. Plans and loans were immediately arranged for the purchase of 2000 kilos of an unwanted foreign seed order, so committed were we to the promise of this commodity. Originally these unwanted acacia seeds were destined for the Middle East where Australian wattles are used for dune stabilisation. Instead the seeds became the spearhead of a genuine future for a wild food industry.

***Acacia victoriae*, commonly known as 'gundabluey' and 'prickly wattle', has a rich coffee-hazelnut flavour and is now my favourite native beverage. The pleasant aroma and flavour easily surpasses that of the best coffee alternatives found commercially. The seed of *Acacia murrayana* is much like that of *Acacia victoriae* in appearance, but with delightfully subtle differences in the flavour. In time, the connoisseur will make a choice of preferred wattle varieties and blends.**

Warwick Kent

grounds are retained which concentrates the strong wattle flavour even more. This paste can be made ahead and stored in the refrigerator or freezer without losing any of its original potency. The flavouring extracted from roasted *Acacia victoriae* is particularly appropriate for dairy products, but does not marry as easily with chocolate.

Recently wattleseed has been added to recipes merely for the sake of using a bush food and unfortunately products have appeared in the marketplace which do not do justice to the incredible power of this natural flavour. Although wattleseed has been successfully incorporated into breads, its flavour has been less effective in biscuits. The latest in the line of quality wattleseed innovations is Nick Chlebnikoski's Wattle Seed Liqueur. The classic swing-top bottle, encased in paperbark, holds an exquisite, dark coffee-style liqueur which can be drunk on the rocks with a cloud of cream or folded through a crème brûlée.

Since my 'discovery' of wattle, I have put it to regular use on the menus of my restaurants. One of the original — and still the most popular — desserts is the Rolled Wattleseed Pavlova. Pavlovas have always been made on each side of the Tasman Sea, with Australia and New Zealand both claiming to have invented the confectionery. A very good pavlova recipe was published in New Zealand in May 1934, and older meringue recipes existed from 1926. Regardless of these facts, Australians maintain that a West Australian chef, Herbert Francis Sasche, created the pavlova in 1935.

The Rolled Wattleseed Pavlova is my contribution to this long, interesting and controversial saga and I have used the distinctive flavour of wattleseed to add a rich Australian character to the filling. The concept of a rolled pavlova was given to me by Don Loncantro, a Sydney man credited with having assisted in developing the instant pavlova mix that has become a familiar sight packaged in its egg-shaped container. The first rolled pavlova appeared in 1979 with a filling of fresh whipped cream and passionfruit pulp.

Wattleseed Liqueur, a product of Witjuti, The Original Australian Bush Tucker.

<'riberries' wattle cappuccino>

- ice-cold, fat-reduced milk
- ½ teaspoon ground coffee
- 'Gundabluey' red label roasted and ground wattleseed
- chocolate powder for sprinkling
- sugar to taste

1. Froth ice-cold milk by steam and rest to set froth.
2. Place a little coffee across the mesh of the espresso machine head, then add 1 heaped tablespoon of wattleseed. Press down and sprinkle a little more coffee across the top.
3. Extract about a nip and a half (45 ml / 1½ fl oz) of wattle brew into a coffee cup.
4. Pour milk to three-quarters fill the cup and spoon froth onto surface. Top with more milk to raise froth level.
5. Sprinkle with chocolate and add sugar to taste.

Note: The coffee is not added to this recipe for its flavour. When hot water is added to ground wattleseeds they swell up and have a tendency to obstruct the fine mesh of the espresso head. The sprinkle of coffee allows the free flow of water through the grounds. To keep the beverage totally free of caffeine a commercial chicory made be substituted for the coffee. Half coffee, half wattle is also a great blend, the wattle giving the coffee a pleasant hazelnut overtone. Wattle is not sweet, but sugar is not vital to its flavour. To obtain great milk froth, ensure the milk is ice-cold and the frothing jug also chilled. Low-fat milk seems to froth best.

< saskia's wattleseed ice cream >

1 can evaporated milk, chilled overnight

110 g (3½ oz) caster sugar (superfine granulated sugar)

2 teaspoons gelatine

2 tablespoons water

150 ml (5 fl oz) cream

2 tablespoons 'Gundabluey' Mud

This recipe was the first attempt to use wattleseed in a culinary application after its espresso debut. The talented young woman who is credited with this magnificent recipe, Saskia Hay, served her apprenticeship at my former restaurant, Rowntrees, The Australian Restaurant. The ice cream, created very late one weekend in 1986, floored everyone. The hazelnut-coffee flavour of wattleseed is particularly good for recipes using dairy products, such as custards, yoghurts and milkshakes. This recipe is well suited to home ice-cream making.

Warwick Kent

Saskia Hay, inventor of the wattleseed ice cream.

1. Whip the evaporated milk until frothy and doubled in volume.
2. Add sugar gradually while beating.
3. Dissolve gelatine in water and add to mixture, still beating.
4. In a separate bowl, whisk the cream until soft peaks form.
5. Fold cream in whipped milk mixture, with 'Gundabluey' Mud.
6. Pour into a tray and freeze immediately, using fast freeze setting if possible.

Warwick Kent

Saskia's wattleseed ice cream.

<rolled wattleseed pavlova>

50 g (2 oz) macadamia nuts, roasted and unsalted

100 g (3½ oz) hazelnuts, roasted

100 g (3½ oz) pecan nuts, roasted

(a) ½ cup caster sugar (superfine granulated sugar)

1 heaped teaspoon cinnamon

6 egg whites

1 teaspoon vinegar or strained lemon juice

(b) 1½ cups caster sugar (superfine granulated sugar)

200 ml (6½ fl oz) cream

2 tablespoons 'Gundabluey' Mud

When making meringues of any sort it is imperative that the mixing bowl and whisks are not greasy. It is also vital that no speck of egg yolk is present with the whites as even a minute amount of yolk is enough fat to prevent the whites from stiffening. An oven at 150°C (300 °F) is the precise temperature for the perfect pavlova. More or less than this heat will dramatically alter the result. Too much added 'Gundabluey' Mud may curdle the cream. If you wish, you can use an emu egg. One emu egg is equivalent to 12 hen eggs, but there is really only enough to make one pavlova. The flavour isn't compromised.

Preheat oven to 150°C (300 °F).

SUGAR CRUST

1. In a food processor, chop macadamia nuts to large crumbs only and set aside.
2. Repeat process with hazelnuts and pecans and set aside.
3. Place sugar *(a)* and cinnamon in food processor and whizz for 15 seconds; add all the set-aside nuts and whizz a further 20 seconds.

MERINGUE

1. Line an open-ended swiss-roll tray with greaseproof paper. Use a little water on the underside of the paper only, to fix it in position.
2. Whisk egg whites with vinegar until soft peaks form.
3. Add half the sugar *(b)* gradually to the whites, whisking until whites are stiff.
4. Fold in the remaining sugar.
5. Empty entire contents of the mixing bowl in one clean sweep, using a rubber spatula, onto the prepared tray. This helps to keep the air pockets to a minimum.
6. Spread the mixture evenly with a goose-neck spatula.
7. Sprinkle crust mixture evenly over the meringue.
8. Bake in the oven at 150°C (300°F) for 20–22 minutes.
9. Remove meringue from oven and place clean tea towel or a large sheet of greaseproof paper over the top and invert onto a cake rack. Allow to cool.
10. Trim the four sides with a serrated knife and carefully remove the greaseproof paper.
12. Whip the fresh cream until it starts to thicken. Add the 'Gundabluey' Mud and continue to whip until stiff.
13. Spread cream evenly over meringue and roll the pavlova like a swiss roll.

Note: This pavlova looks sensational when decorated with sugarbark (see recipe in Chapter 6, page 66).

Warwick Kent

Rolled wattleseed pavlova.

<'gundabluey' mud>

110 g (3½ oz) 'Gundabluey' red label roasted and ground wattleseed

600 ml (1 pint / 20 fl oz) water

pinch salt

The mud is made from the absorption of water by the roasted ground wattleseeds over a very low flame. It is important never to boil the seeds as the flavour becomes 'dusty' and bitter. The mud stores well in the refrigerator and will tolerate freezing.

1. Cook wattleseed with water and salt in an open stainless-steel frying pan to allow quick evaporation. Do not boil.
2. Simmer, reducing volume by two-thirds, or until the grounds meet the surface of the liquid.
3. Blend the cooked grounds in a blender at high speed until they become a smooth mud.
4. Scrape the contents of the blender into a clean container, cool and seal.
5. Store in the refrigerator.

Warwick Kent

Gundabluey Mud.

bibliography

Illawarra Plum

Brand Millar, J., et al., *Tables of Composition of Australian Aboriginal Foods*, Aboriginal Studies Press, Canberra, for the Australian Institute of Aboriginal and Torres Strait Islander Studies, 1993.

Costermans, L., *Native Trees and Shrubs of South Eastern Australia*, Lansdowne (Weldon), Sydney, 1992.

Fuller, L., *Wollongong's Native Trees*, Weston & Co, Kiama, 1982.

Organ, M., *Illawarra and South Coast Aborigines 1770–1850*, Aboriginal Education Unit, Wollongong University, 1990.

Robinson, L., *Field Guide to the Native Plants of Sydney*, Kangaroo Press, Sydney, 1991.

Kangaroo & Wallaby

Aboriginal Lands Council, *Support Kangaroo Meat For Human Consumption: Relating to Meat Industry (Game Meat) Amendment Act 1992*, from the office of the Minister for Agriculture and Rural Affairs, document dated 18 November 1992.

Australian Museum, *Complete Book of Australian Mammals*, ed. R. Strahan, Angus & Robertson, Sydney, 1983.

Barrett, C., *Wildlife in Australia Illustrated*, Colourgravure Publications, Melbourne, no date.

Berndt, R.M. & C.H., *The World of the First Australians*, Ure Smith, Sydney, 1964.

Berndt, R.M. & C.H., *Man, Land and Myth in North Australia*, Ure Smith, Sydney, 1970.

Greenway, J., *Down Among the Wild Men*, Hutchinson Group, Richmond, Vic., 1973.

Grzimek, B., *Four-Legged Australians, Adventures with Animals and Men in Australia*, trans. J. Maxwell Brownjohn, Collins, London, 1967.

Horton, D. (gen. ed.), *Encyclopaedia of Aboriginal Australia*, vol. 1., Aboriginal Studies Press, Canberra, for the Australian Institute of Aboriginal and Torres Strait Islander Studies, 1994.

Langloh Parker, K., *Australian Legendary Tales*, ed. H. Drake-Brockman, Angus & Robertson, Sydney, 1953.

Lenah Game Meats of Tasmania, *A Chef's Guide*, brochure, no date.

New South Wales, *Meat Industry (Game Meat) Amendment Act 1992*, no. 85.

New South Wales, *Meat Industry Act 1978*, no. 54.

Southern Game Meats, *Kangaroo the Taste of Australia*, brochure, no date.

Sydney Morning Herald, 2 April 1993, letters to the editor.

Troughton, E., *Furred Animals of Australia*, Angus & Robertson, Sydney, 1941.

Native Pepper

Brown, R., *Prodromus Florae Novae Hollandiae, et Insulae Van Diemen*, vol. 2 (manuscript, 1830), facsimile edition, Hapner Publishing Co, New York, 1960.

Cribb, A.B. & J.W., *Wild Medicine in Australia*, Fontana (Collins), Sydney, 1981.

Essential Oils of Tasmania, product specification and technical data for *Tasmannia lanceolata*, company paper, unpublished, no date.

Farquhar, Ian, private interview with author, 3 October 1995.

Hannan, Rory, & Woodley, Charles (of Tasmanian Wilderness Foliage), personal communication to author, 21 March 1993.

James, P., private correspondence to Mr Stephen Harris, 21 May 1990.

James, P., processing notes for salt-dried pepperberries (*Tasmannia lanceolata*), Gundabluey Bushfoods Notes, unpublished, 1993.

Read, C. (of Diemen Pepper), private correspondence to author, regarding *Tasmannia lanceolata*, 3 October 1995.

State Library of New South Wales, *A Fine Field for Botanizing*, exhibition catalogue, Library Council of NSW, 1981.

Toussaint-Samat, M., *A History of Food*, trans. Anthea Bell, Blackwell, Oxford, 1994.

Bunya Bunya

Aurousseau, M. (ed.), *The Letters of F.W. Ludwig Leichhardt*, vol. II, Second Series, no. CXXXIV, Cambridge University Press for the Hakluyt Society, London, 1968.

Boland, D.J., et al., *Forest Trees of Australia*, Thomas Nelson, Melbourne, 1984.

Cribb, A.B. & J.W., *Wild Food in Australia*, revd edn, Fontana (Collins), Sydney, 1987.

Petrie, C.C., *Tom Petrie's Reminiscences of Early Queensland*, Watson, Ferguson & Co, Brisbane, 1904.

Russell, H.S., *Genesis of Queensland*, 1888. (Mitchell Library Collection.)

Sydney Morning Herald, 9 June 1906, 18 June 1906, 20 June 1906, letters to the editor from J.H. Maiden and C. Campbell Petrie.

Witjuti Grub

Brand Millar, J., et al., *Tables of Composition of Australian Aboriginal Foods*, Aboriginal Studies Press, Canberra, for the Australian Institute of Aboriginal and Torres Strait Islander Studies, 1993.

Commonwealth Scientific and Industrial Research Organisation, Division of Entomology, *The Insects of Australia*, Melbourne University Press, Melbourne, 1970.

Hooke, H., 'Fine Wine', *Sydney Morning Herald*, 23 May 1995.

Horton, D. (gen. ed.), *Encyclopaedia of Aboriginal Australia*, vol. 2, Aboriginal Studies Press, Canberra, for Aboriginal Institute of Aboriginal and Torres Strait Islander Studies, 1994.

Irvine, G., 'Putting Insects on the Australian Menu', *Food Australia*, vol. 41, no. 1, January 1989, pages 565–6.

Red Quandong

Barker, R. (ed.), *Australian Food Plant Study Group Newsletter*, no. 3, April 1985.

Commonwealth Scientific and Industrial Research Organisation, Division of Horticultural Research, 'Technical Notes: Preliminary Assessment of an Orchard of Quandong Seedling Trees', CSIRO Published Paper 607, reproduced in *Journal of the Australian Institute of Agricultural Science*, vol. 48, 1982.

Cribb, A.B. & J.W., *Wild Food in Australia*, revd edn, Fontana (Collins), Sydney, 1987.

Curtis, B.V., 'Spare a Spot for the Santalum', *Australian Plants: Santalaceae* (Journal of the Society for Growing Australian Native Plants), vol. 7, June 1974.

Edwards, W.H., 'Plants in Pitjantjatjara Life and Mythology', *SGAP Seminar Papers*, Society for Growing Australian Plants, Adelaide, 1983.

Fairley, A., *A Complete Guide to Warrumbungle National Parks*, Child & Henry, Brookvale, NSW, 1983.

Ferguson, M., personal communications to the author, 1989–95.

Grant, W.J.R., & Buttrose, M.S., 'Santalum Fruit', *Australian Plants* (Journal of the Society for Growing Australian Native Plants), vol. 9, no. 75, June 1978.

Lamont, H., & Powell, B., *Quandongs*, brochure, Tree Facts series, State Tree Centre, South Australia, February 1993.

Maiden, J.H., *The Useful Australian Native Plants (Including Tasmania)* (1889), facsimile edition, Compendium Pty Ltd, Melbourne, 1975.

Possingham, J., 'Young, Old and New Crops: Macadamias, Pistachios and Quandongs', a paper presented to the Second Symposium of Australian Gastronomy, Adelaide, 1985.

Shineberg, Dorothy, *They Came for Sandalwood*, Melbourne University Press, Melbourne, 1967.

Emu

Australian Encyclopaedia, Australian Geographic Publication, Sydney, 1988.

Eastman, M., *The Life of the Emu*, Angus & Robertson, Sydney, 1969.

Frauca, H., *Birds from the Seas, Swamps and Scrubs of Australia*, Heinemann, Melbourne, 1967.

Leichhardt, L., *Journal of an Overland Expedition in Australia, From Moreton to Port Essington, A Distance of Upwards of 3,000 miles, during the Years 1844–1845*, T & W Boone, London, 1847.

Manning, R., 'Emu Farming in NSW', *NPW News* (National Parks & Wildlife Service), December 1995, page 9.

Marchant, S., & Higgins, P.J. (eds), *Handbook of Australian, New Zealand and Antarctic Birds*, vol. 1: *Ratites to Ducks* (pt A), Oxford University Press, Melbourne, 1990.

Renshaw, G., 'The Black Emu, Society for the Preservation of the Empire', *Journal of the Royal Geographic Society of Australia*, South Australian Branch, vol.27, 1925–26, pp.17–22.

Smetana, P., *Emu Farming: Background Information*, Western Australian Department of Agriculture, March 1993.

Western Australia, Department of Agriculture, *Register of Approved Emu Cuts and Items*, June 1993.

Barramundi

Allen, G.R., *Freshwater Fishes of Australia*, TFH Publication, Brookvale, NSW, 1989.

Grant, E.M., *Guide to Fishes*, Queensland Department of Harbours and Marine, Brisbane, 1978.

Healy, T., *A Review of the East Coast Barramundi Fishery and Proposed Management Measures*, Discussion Paper, Queensland Fish Management Authority, no date.

Merrick, J.R., & Schmida, G.E., *Australian Freshwater Fishes, Biology and Management*, Griffin Press, 1984.

Queensland, Department of Primary Industries, *The Facts About Barramundi*, Leaflet QL 86030, no date.

Queensland Fish Management Authority, *Management Changes in the East Coast Barramundi Fishery*, June 1992.

Thomson, D., *Donald Thomson in Arnhem Land*, comp. Nicolas Peterson, Currey O'Neil Ross, Melbourne, 1983.

Magpie Goose & Cape Barren Goose

Davis, S. & Ganambar, *Lawuk, Dharrathbarra, Arnhemland Environ*, book 3, Milingimbi Literature Production Centre, 1978.

Egecombe, J., *Discovering Flinders Island*, J. Egecombe, Sydney. 1992.

Firth, H.J., *Waterfowl in Australia*, Angus & Robertson, Sydney, 1976; Australian Natural Science edn, 1982.

Manolis, C. (of Wildlife International Research, Crocadillis Park, Northern Territory), personal communication to Janet Bruce, October 1995.

Marchant, S., & Higgins, P.J. (eds), *Handbook of Australian, New Zealand and Antarctic Birds*, vol. 1: *Ratites to Ducks* (pt B), Oxford University Press, Melbourne, 1990.

Morrison, A.B., & Purling, T.J., A Report to the Western Australian Department of Fisheries and Wildlife, Covering Observations on Cape Barren Geese, Held at the Poultry Research Station, Woodlands, WA, from mid 1978 until April 1982 (unpublished report).

National Parks and Wildlife Service of Tasmania, *Cape Barren Goose, Cereopsis novaehollandiae*, brochure, September 1987.

Northern Territory, Department of Conservation, Hunting Regulations for the 1995 Northern Territory Waterfowl Hunting Season.

Rhodes, C., Proposal for Farming Cape Barren Geese, unpublished paper, no date.

Tasmania, Department of Primary Industry, Draft Code of Practice for the Welfare of Animals Farmed: Cape Barren Geese, October 1995.

Sharland, M., 'The Wild Geese of Darwin', in *Stories of Australian Birds*, ed. G. Pizzey, Currey O'Neil, Melbourne, 1983.

Thomson, D., *Donald Thomson in Arnhem Land*, comp. Nicolas Peterson, Currey O'Neil Ross, Melbourne, 1983.

Whitehead, P.J., 'Magpie Geese, Mangoes and Sustainable Development', *Australian Natural History* (Journal of the Australian Museum), vol. 23, no. 10, Spring 1991, page 785.

Barks & Fuels

Boland, D.J., et al., *Forest Trees of Australia*, Thomas Nelson, Melbourne, 1984.

Brendt, R.M. & C.H., *The World of the First Australians*, Ure Smith, Sydney, 1977.

Cribb, A.W. & J.W., *Useful Wild Plants in Australia*, Collins, Sydney, 1982.

Edwards, R., *Aboriginal Bark Canoes of the Murray Valley*, Rigby, Adelaide, 1972.

Harney, B., *Bill Harney's Cook Book*, Lansdowne Press, Melbourne, 1960.

Horton, D. (gen. ed.), *Encyclopaedia of Aboriginal Australia*, vol. 2, Aboriginal Studies Press, Canberra, for Aboriginal Institute of Aboriginal and Torres Strait Islander Studies, 1994.

Low, T., *Bush Medicine: A Pharmacopoeia of Natural Remedies*, Angus & Robertson, Sydney, 1990.

Maiden, J.H., *The Useful Australian Native Plants (Including Tasmania)* (1889), facsimile edition, Compendium Pty Ltd, Melbourne, 1975.

Turbet, P., *The Aborigines of the Sydney District Before 1788*, Kangaroo Press, Sydney, 1989.

Sharks & Rays

Alston, A., Close, I., Gilbert, P.W. et al., *Sharks: Silent Hunters of the Deep*, Reader's Digest, Sydney, 1986.

Davis, S.L., & Prescott, J.R.V., *Aboriginal Frontiers and Boundaries in Australia*, Melbourne University Press, Melbourne, 1992.

Stevens, J.D., & Paxton, J.R., 'Shark Attack: But Who's the Victim', *Australian Natural History* (Journal of the Australian Museum), vol. 24, no. 3, Summer 1992–3, page 46.

Beaglehole, J.C., *The Journals of Captain James Cook: The Voyage of the Endeavour, 1768–1771*, Cambridge University Press for the Hakluyt Society, London, 1968.

Last, P.R., & Stevens, J.D., *Sharks and Rays of Australia*, CSIRO Publications, Melbourne, 1994.

Marshall, N.A., *The Life of Fishes*, Weidenfeld & Nicholson, London, 1965.

O'Brian, P., *Joseph Banks, A Life: Explorer, Plant Hunter, Scientist*, Collins Harvill, London, 1988.

Tetragon & Saltbushes

Anderson, J., 'Account of a New Esculent Vegetable', *Curtis's Botanical Magazine*, vol. 172.

Clark, C.M.H. (ed.), *Sources of Australian History* (Joseph Banks Recommends Botany Bay as a Site For a Convict Colony, 1779, from Journals of the House of Commons, vol. xxxvii), Oxford University Press, London, 1971.

Low, T., *Wild Foods Plants of Australia*, Angus & Robertson, Sydney, 1988.

Maiden, J.H., *The Useful Australian Native Plants (Including Tasmania)* (1889), facsimile edition, Compendium Pty Ltd, Melbourne, 1975.

O'Brian, P., *Joseph Banks, A Life: Explorer, Plant Hunter, Scientist*, Collins Harvill, London, 1988.

Reed, A.W., *Captain Cook in Australia*, Reed.

Sturtevant, E.L., *Sturtevant's Notes on Edible Plant*s, New York, 1919.

White, J., *Journal of A Voyage to New South Wales* (1790), Angus & Robertson, Sydney, 1962.

Herbs, Spices & Oils

Archer, D.W. (of Toona Essential Oils Pty Ltd), personal communication, to author, 7 November 1995.

Archer, D.W., personal communication to Gundabluey Bushfoods, 28 November 1994.

Colwell, M., *The Voyages of Matthew Flinders*, Paul Hamlyn, Sydney, 1970.

Cribb, A.B. & J.W., *Wild Medicine in Australia*, Fontana (Collins), 1984.

Low, T., *Bush Tucker: Australia's Wild Food Harvest*, Angus & Robertson, Sydney, 1989.

Maiden, J.H., *The Useful Australian Native Plants (Including Tasmania)* (1889), facsimile edition, Compendium Pty Ltd, Melbourne, 1975.

Macadamia

Australian Macadamia Society, *Macadamia Industry Outline*, brochure, Lismore, NSW, 1995.

Australian Macadamia Society, *The Macadamia Story*, brochure, Lismore, NSW, 1992.

Erlich, R., 'Mad About the Mac', *The Australian Way* (Qantas Inflight Magazine), Qantas, Sydney, December 1994.

Hawaiian Annual Magazine, 1928, pages 95–8, articles 'Widening Our Industries', 'Macadamia Nut Culture', and 'Hawaiian Nut Culture'.

Kraus, B., *Bibliography of the Macadamia*, Hawaii Agricultural Experimental Station, College of Tropical Agriculture, University of Hawaii, Honolulu, 1970–72.

Mueller, F., *Account of Some New Australian Plants*, Philosophical Institute of Victoria, 5 August 1857.

Queensland, Department of Primary Industries, *Is Macadamia Growing For You*, Queensland Department of Primary Industries, 1990.

Rakusan, E., personal communication to author, 6 January 1996.

Swain, M., 'Some Impressions and an Object Lesson From Honolulu', *Herself Magazine*, 1 November 1928.

Wrigley, J.W., & Fagg, M., *Australian Native Plants: A Manual for the Propagation, Cultivation and Use*, William Collins, Sydney, 1979.

Cider Gum, Sugarbag & Hard Yacca

Adams, Jane, 'She'll be Apples, by Gum', *The Bulletin*, 1 May 1990.

Gott, B., & Conran, J., *Victorian Koorie Plants*, Yangennanock Women's Group, Hamilton, Victoria, 1991.

Harris, S., 'Three Tasmanian Plants with Potential for Commercial Development as Sources of Bush Foods', a paper presented to the Fifth Symposium of Australian Gastronomy, Adelaide, 1990.

Isaacs, J., Bush Food: *Aboriginal Food and Herbal Medicine*, Weldons, Sydney, 1987.

Maiden, J.H., *The Useful Australian Native Plants (Including Tasmania)* (1889), facsimile edition, Compendium Pty Ltd, Melbourne, 1975.

Mollison, B., & Everitt, C., *The Tasmanian Aborigines and Their Descendants, Chronology, Genealogies and Social Data*, pt 2, Whitemark Historical Society, Flinders Island, Tas., December 1978.

Reed, A.W. (ed.), *Aboriginal Words of Australia*, Reed, Frenchs Forest, NSW, 1965.

Smyth, R., *Aborigines of Australia*, 2 vols, Government Printer, Melbourne, 1878.

Sweet Berries & Sour Fruits

Bodkin, F., *Encyclopaedia Botanica: The Essential Reference Guide to Native and Exotic Plants in Australia*, Angus & Robertson, Sydney, 1986.

Cooper, W., *Fruit of the Rainforest: A Guide to Fruits of the Australian Tropical Rainforest*, RD Press for GEO, Chatswood, NSW, 1994.

Cribb, A.B. & J.W., *Wild Food in Australia*, revd edn, Fontana (Collins), Sydney, 1987.

Flannery, T., *The Future Eaters*, Reed Books, Chatswood, NSW, 1994.

Flood, J., *Archaeology of the Dreamtime: The Story of Prehistoric Australia and its People*, William Collins, Sydney, 1983.

Gott, B., & Conran, J., *Victorian Koorie Plants*, Yangennanock Women's Group, Hamilton, Victoria, 1991.

Hardwick, P., personal communication to author, 1987.

Low, T., *Bush Tucker: Australia's Wild Food Harvest*, Angus & Robertson, Sydney, 1989.

Miller, D., 'Bush Tucker, an Opportunity for the Small Farmer', Grass Roots, no. 111, Oct-Nov 1995.

Peverill, M., personal communication to author, 1995.

Robson, L., *A History of Tasmania*, vol. 1, Oxford University Press, Melbourne, 1983.

South Australia, Department of Environment and Natural Resources, *Collection of Seed From Native Plants in South Australia*, May 1995.

Vandepeer, J., personal communication to author, 1995.

Marron, Koonac & Gilgies

Morrissy, N.M., 'Aquaculture of Marron, *Cherax tenuimanus*, Part 1: Site Selection and the Potential of Marron for Aquaculture', *Fisheries Research Bulletin*, no. 17, Western Australian Marine Research Laboratories, Perth, Western Australia, 1976.

New South Wales Department of Agriculture, *Guidelines for Avoiding Cruelty in Shellfish Preparation: The Humane Treatment of Crustaceans in the Restaurant and Catering Industries*, brochure, no date.

Rose, M. (of Animal Ethics Committee), personal communication to author, January 1996.

Suisman, J. (of Flying Squid Brothers), personal communication to author, 1994.

Western Australia, Department of Fisheries, *Aquaculture WA*, no. 2, Western

Australian Department of Fisheries, 1995.
Western Australia, Department of Fisheries, *Biology and Farming of the Yabbie*, Western Australian Department of Fisheries, no date.
Western Australia, Department of Fisheries and Wildlife, *Marron of Western Australia*, Fisheries Education Publication no. 2, Western Australian Department of Fisheries and Wildlife, Perth, 1985.
Western Australia, Department of Fisheries, *Identifying Freshwater Crayfish*, Western Australian Department of Fisheries, March 1993.
Western Australia, Department of Fisheries, *Marron and Marron Farming*, Fisheries Information Publication no. 4, Extension and Publicity Office, Western Australian Department of Fisheries, Perth, 1985.

Yolla

Adam-Smith, P., *Moonbird People*, Rigby, Adelaide, 1965.
Blakers, M., Davies, S.J.J.F., & Reilly, P.N., *The Atlas of Australian Birds*, Royal Australian Ornithologists Union and Melbourne University Press, Melbourne, 1984.
DeJose, J., *Australian Coastal Birds in Colour*, Reed Books, Sydney, 1984.
Hooper, R.H., *King Island Story*, ed. Mark Richmond, Peko-Wallsend Ltd, Sydney, 1973.
Hope, J., 'Wildlife of Bass Strait', in *Bass Strait: Australia's Last Frontier*, ed. S. Murray-Smith, ABC Books, Sydney, 1987.
Murray-Smith, S., 'Bass Strait: Discovery and Exploration', in *Bass Strait: Australia's Last Frontier*, ed. S. Murray-Smith, ABC Books, Sydney, 1987.
Reeves, E., article in Lifestyle Section, *Hobart Mercury*, 6 October 1993.
Serventy, D.L., Serventy, V., & Warham, J., *The Handbook of Australian Sea-Birds*, A.H. & A.W. Reed, Sydney, 1971.
Serventy, D.L., 'Mutton-birding', in *Bass Strait: Australia's Last Frontier*, ed. S. Murray-Smith, ABC Books, Sydney, 1987.
Skira, I.J., 'Human Exploitation of the Short-tailed Shearwater (*Puffinus tenuirostris*)', *Papers and Proceedings of the Royal Society of Tasmania*, vol. 124, no. 1, 1990.
Skira, I.J., 'The Short-tailed Shearwater: A Review of its Biology', *Australian Bird Reviews*, no. 3., reprinted from *Corella*, vol. 15, no. 2, 1991.
Skira, I.J., 'Tasmanian Aboriginals and Muttonbirding, an Historical Examination', PhD thesis, University of Tasmania, Hobart, September 1993.
Skira, I., 'A Muttonbird in the Hand', *Natural History* (USA), August, 1995.
Smith, T., 'Sinking of the "Sydney Cove" put Tasmania on the Map', *GEO* (Australasia), vol. 17, no. 1, Jan-Feb 1995.
Woodward, D.R., et al., in collaboration with Tasmanian Aboriginal Centre, 'Nutritional Analysis of the Flesh and Oil of Yolla, the Tasmania Mutton Bird *Puffinus tenuirostris*: A Useful Source of Omega–3 Polyunsaturated Fatty Acids', *Australian Journal of Nutrition and Dietetics*, vol. 52, no. 2, June 1995.
Yolla Promotions, Tasmanian Aboriginal Centre Inc., circular, no date.

Oysters, Periwinkles & Mussels

Davis, S.L., & Prescott, J.R.V., *Aboriginal Frontiers and Boundaries in Australia*, Melbourne University Press, Melbourne, 1992.
Flood, J., *Archaeology of the Dreamtime: The Story of Prehistoric Australia and its People*, William Collins, Sydney, 1983.
Gould League of Victoria, *Coastal Wildlife*, Gould League, Melbourne, 1983.
Haddon, F., *Environmental Field Guide to Flora and Fauna, Australia's Seashore*, Simon & Schuster, Sydney, 1992.
Holliday, J.E., & Nell, J.A., *Pacific Oysters in New South Wales*, 2nd edn, Agfact F2.1.3, New South Wales Department of Agriculture and Fisheries, 1990.
Horton, D. (gen. ed.), *The Encyclopaedia of Aboriginal Australia*, vol. 2, Aboriginal Studies Press, Canberra, for Australian Institute of Australian and Torres Strait Islander Studies, 1994.
Hughes, R., *The Fatal Shore*, Pan Books, London, 1987.
Malcolm, W.B., *The Sydney Rock Oyster*, Agfact F3.1.1, New South Wales Department of Agriculture, 1987.
Tasmania, Department of Primary Industry, *Draft Interim Management Plan for the Periwinkle Fishery*, 1991.
Toussaint-Samat, M., *A History of Food*, trans. Anthea Bell, Blackwell, Oxford, 1994.
Travers, R., *The Tasmanians, The Story of a Doomed Race*, Cassell Australia, Melbourne, 1968.
Turbet, P., *The Aborigines of the Sydney District Before 1788*, Kangaroo Press, Sydney, 1989.
White, J., *Journal of a Voyage to New South Wales* (1790), Angus & Robertson, Sydney, 1962.

Billy-goat Plum

Brand Millar, J., et al., *Tables of Composition of Australian Aboriginal Foods*, Aboriginal Studies Press, Canberra, for the Australian Institute of Aboriginal and Torres Strait Islander Studies, 1993.
Cherikoff, V.,personal communication to author, August 1991.
Hiddens, L., personal communication to author, September 1991.
Isaacs, J., *Bush Food: Aboriginal Food and Herbal Medicine*, Weldons, Sydney, 1987.
Low, T., *Bush Medicine: A Pharmacopoeia of Natural Remedies*, Angus & Robertson, Sydney, 1990.
Woods, B., personal communications to author, September 1991 and December 1995.

Wattleseed

Basham, F.G., *Aunt Daisy's Cookery Book of Selected Recipes, Broadcast by Aunt Daisy*, Radio NZ, New Zealand, 1935.
Brand, J., & Maggiore, P., 'The Nutritional Composition of Australian Acacia seeds', in *Australia Dry-Zone Acacia For Human Food*, eds A.P.N. House & C.E. Harwood, Commonwealth Scientific and Industrial Research Organisation, Division of Forestry, 1992.
Brand Millar, J., et al., *Tables of Composition of Australian Aboriginal Foods*, Aboriginal Studies Press, Canberra, for the Australian Institute of Aboriginal and Torres Strait Islander Studies, 1993.
Burton, D., 'Conflict and Spanish Wind: Pavlova's Saga', *Evening Post* (NZ), 3 July 1985.
Cowell, R.E., personal communication to author, 19 April 1990.
Devitt, J., 'Acacias: A Traditional Aboriginal Food Source in Central Australia,' in *Australia Dry-Zone Acacia For Human Food*, eds A.P.N. House & C.E. Harwood, Commonwealth Scientific and Industrial Research Organisation, Division of Forestry, 1992.
Home Journal, 13 July 1934, A Page or Two for Women: 'Request Pavlova Cake'.
New South Wales Egg Corporation, recipe for Pavola Roll, no date.
Otago Daily Times, 2 May 1974, Mainly For Women Column: 'Australian Claim On Pavlova Unsupported By N.Z. Evidence'.
Schmitt, H., 'The Man Who Whipped Up the World's First Pavlova', *Woman's Day*, 27 August 1973.
Thomson, L., 'Australia's Subtropical Dry-zone Acacia Species with Human Food Potential,' in *Australia Dry-Zone Acacia For Human Food*, eds A.P.N. House & C.E. Harwood, Commonwealth Scientific and Industrial Research Organisation, Division of Forestry, 1992.
Weller, Margaret M., personal communication to author, 16 May 1990.
Wistrand, J., personal communication to author, 11 June 1990.
World Book Encyclopedia (1979 edn), vol. 24, page 794.

Index

A

B

C

D

S

T

V

W

where to buy ingredients

australia

CHEF'S WAREHOUSE
252 Riley Street,
Surry Hills NSW 2010
Tel: 61 2 9211 4555

DAVID JONES AUSTRALIA LTD
Food Glorious Food
Selected stores throughout
Australia

GUNDABLUEY PTY LTD
Wholesalers of Wattleseed, Lemon Myrtle, Native Peppers and other quality native food products.
For further information please send self-addressed envelope to:

Gundabluey Consumer Services
PO Box 500,
Epping NSW 2121
Australia
ph: 61 2 9316 6300
fax: 61 2 9316 6305

united kingdom

FOOD SOURCE
In association with
Parmigiani Figlio Limited
London UK
Tel/Fax: 44 171 376 1890